The Essential Fan Guide to

THE GOLDEN GIRLS

The Essential Fan Guide to

THE GOLDEN GIRLS

EMMA LEWIS

Illustrations by CHANTEL DE SOUSA

Smith
Street
Books

Introducing

The Golden Girls

Picture this: NBC Studios, September 1985.
Enter stage left Bea Arthur, Rue McClanahan, Betty
White and Estelle Getty. Take an amazing scriptwriting
team, and expert production and direction, and what
do you get? One of TV's best loved and most
respected sitcoms of all time.

The weekly adventures of Dorothy Zbornak, Blanche Devereaux, Rose Nylund and Sophia Petrillo were an instant hit with audiences, and filled a gap in the market for TV content about the experiences of older women. It was an entirely new TV concept to watch four older women navigate dating, relationships, ageing and sometimes the task of simply making ends meet.

The Golden Girls brought an exciting new brand of situation comedy to audiences around the world, and everyone from young to old were watching – children were drawn to Sophia's hilarious one-liners and antics, while more mature audiences enjoyed the wit of Dorothy, the outrageousness of Blanche and the hilarious innocence of Rose.

The show was such a hit that seven seasons were filmed between 1985 and 1992. *The Golden Girls* was still rating well in 1992, and only came to an end because Bea Arthur was ready to move on and wanted the show to end on a high. The characters were so beloved that a spin-off, *The Golden Palace*, was concocted; however it lasted only a single season.

Fast-forward to three decades later and audiences are still in love with *The Golden Girls*. Seldom out of syndication since its first airing, it remains one of the most adored American sitcoms of all time. Unlike many others of a certain vintage, *The Golden Girls* has survived the ageing process and is still funny and relevant to audiences today.

This book is written as a field guide to *The Golden Girls* and as a nod to the incredible talent of four amazing women and a superbly talented cast and crew. It is dedicated in loving memory to those *Golden Girls* who are no longer with us, and to the inner Golden Girl inside all of us.

How it All Began

It's 1984 in Burbank, California. A group of television executives are attending a TV special at NBC's Warner Bros. studios, and two older actors grace the stage: Selma Diamond (1920–1985) of *Night Court* fame, and Doris Roberts (1925–2016) from *Remington Steele* (and later, *Everybody Loves Raymond*). The women perform a skit from a fictional sitcom called *Miami Nice,* a show about older people living in Miami parodying the NBC success story *Miami Vice*. The skit gets big laughs, and inspires NBC Senior Vice President Warren Littlefield to consider a TV comedy about wisecracking older women.

At the same time, producers Paul Junger Witt and Tony Thomas were pitching to NBC with another idea. Littlefield wasn't convinced by it, and instead suggested they deliver a pilot along the lines of *Miami Nice*. Junger Witt asked his wife Susan Harris (already an accomplished sitcom writer) to work with them, and so she wrote the pilot script. Littlefield liked what he read and a pilot was commissioned.

A strong ensemble cast was required, and the first role to be cast was that of Sophia Petrillo. While Estelle Getty was a relative unknown on television, she had impressed the showrunners with her hit performance in the Off-Broadway show *Torch Song Trilogy*. Next to be cast were the roles of Blanche Devereaux and Rose Nylund. Serendipitously, *Mama's Family* had just been cancelled, and its stars Betty White and Rue McClanahan were now out of work. It's hard to believe that McClanahan was initially cast as Rose and White was cast as Blanche, until the pilot episode director Jay Sandrich decisively swapped the roles late in the piece.

The final role to be cast was that of Dorothy Zbornak. Susan Harris wrote the role with someone like Bea Arthur in mind, and while it is hard to imagine anyone else but Arthur playing Dorothy, the original plan was for Broadway star Elaine Stritch (1925–2014) to play the role. Unfortunately for Stritch,

her audition was a flop, and the showrunners soon approached Arthur, who at first was not convinced – but McClanahan (with whom she had worked with previously on *Maude*) dropped her a line and persuaded her to read for the part.

Once the cast had been assembled, the pilot episode was recorded over two shoots on 17 April 1985. The pilot tested very well with audiences, and the studio had high hopes for the show. *The Golden Girls* premiered on NBC on 14 September 1985, and from its first episode was a ratings success. In its first season, *The Golden Girls* aired on Saturday nights at 9 pm, a time slot that wasn't traditionally high rating. But NBC wanted to screen the show at a time when its aged-over-fifty target audience would likely be home and looking for entertainment. It was evident early on that the gamble had paid off.

A second season was soon commissioned, and from that point on, the successful future of *The Golden Girls* was ensured. Throughout its seven seasons, *The Golden Girls* maintained a sizeable audience, often winning its timeslot. By 1991, the show was still faring well in ratings, but Arthur had decided to call it quits. Arthur chose to leave on her own terms while the show was still at the top of its game, and although the rest of the cast wanted to stay on, the fate of *The Golden Girls* in its current form was sealed.

The final episode aired on 9 May 1992. McClanahan, White and Getty moved on to the ultimately unsuccessful spin-off *The Golden Palace*, but *The Golden Girls* continued to have a life of its own.

From July 1989, NBC aired daytime reruns of the show until September 1990. At this time, syndicated reruns began airing, distributed by Buena Vista Television. In 1997, the Lifetime cable network acquired the exclusive rights to *The Golden Girls* for the next decade or so. In 2009, the Hallmark Channel and

WE tv acquired rights to the show, and since 2013, *The Golden Girls* has been run by TV Land and Logo TV. Since 2017, *The Golden Girls* has been streaming on Hulu.

There have also been several remakes of *The Golden Girls*, based on the original concept, developed all around the world. Some have been more successful than others, but none have compared to the popularity of the original franchise.

The Golden Girls foreign versions include:

An early 1990s Philippines version called *50 Carats, O Di Ba?* (*50 Carats, Or What?*).

In 1993, a British version called *Brighton Belles* was made, but was cancelled early in its first season due to poor ratings.

In 1995, Portugal made *Queridas e Maduras* (*Dear Mature Girls*) that aired for two seasons in 1995 and 1996.

There have been two Spanish versions of the show; *Juntas, Pero No Revueltas*' (Together, But Not Mixed) from the mid-90s and *Las Chicas de Oro* (The Golden Girls) in 2010.

A Russian version called *Bolshie Devochki* (*Big Girls*) was made in 2006, and lasted 32 episodes.

A Greek version, *Chrysa Koritsia* (*Golden Girls*), was made in 2008, and a Dutch version (*Golden Girls*) premiered in 2012.

In 2009, Turkey produced *Altin Kizlar* (*Girls of Gold*), but it only lasted a single episode.

An Israeli version called *Bnot HaZahav* aired from 2011 to 2016.

A 2015 adaptation in Chile called *Los Años Dorados* (*The Golden Years*) sees four retired women living in Viña del Mar.

Getting to Know the Girls

Blanche

Blanche Elizabeth Marie Devereaux (née Hollingsworth) was born in Atlanta, Georgia, to Curtis 'Big Daddy' Hollingsworth and Elizabeth-Ann 'Big Momma' Margaret Bennett Hollingsworth on 29 November, 1932. Blanche was brought up Baptist with her four siblings in her parents' mansion, Twin Oaks. Blanche has an older sister, Charmaine, and older brother, Tad, and two younger siblings, Clayton and Virginia. An accomplished cheerleader and debutante, Blanche attended Miss McIver's Finishing School and was an Alpha Gamma Delta at college.

Blanche was very popular with the gents, and always had a date lined up for Saturday nights. During her senior year in high school, she almost eloped with the father of her cheerleading rival, but thankfully the marriage didn't go ahead. Blanche is also rumoured to have once slept with Elvis Presley in a Motel 6 outside Chattanooga, though according to Blanche it was very dark and there were many young men in Chattanooga back then called Elvis who had mutton-chop sideburns.

Blanche fell madly in love with George Devereaux after meeting him at a university club cotillion. They soon married and had five children: Janet, Rebecca, Doug, Matthew and Biff. Blanche and George were very happily married for decades before his death in 1981.

Blanche and George had moved to Miami just before George passed away, leaving Blanche alone and looking for roommates in an unfamiliar city. *The Golden Girls* house actually belongs to Blanche, who rents out the other rooms to Dorothy, Sophia and Rose.

Always focused on her next conquest, Blanche is the glamorous sex-kitten of the house. She loves to overshare the sordid details of the evening before, and although the other girls tease her, everyone loves to listen in and hear all about the previous night's escapades.

When Dorothy married Lucas Hollingsworth (Blanche's uncle) and moved with him to Atlanta, Sophia, Rose and Blanche decided to try their luck in the hotel business, opening the Golden Palace Hotel in Miami, with Blanche taking on the role of managing the hotel.

*My mother survived
a slight stroke,
which left her,
if I can be frank,
a complete burden.*

Getting to Know the Girls

Dorothy

Dorothy Zbornak (née Petrillo) was born in 1930 on a pinochle table at McSoley's Bar in Brooklyn, New York to Sophia and Salvadore Petrillo. According to Sophia, Dorothy was the tallest baby in Brooklyn and had a rash on her head for the first two years. Dorothy has two siblings, Phil and Gloria.

A high achiever at school, Dorothy became a school teacher, first in New York and then in Miami. While she excelled academically, Dorothy was not so lucky in love. As a teenager, Dorothy thought she was stood up at the prom until she found out many years later that Sophia had scared her date away after he was disrespectful to her. Dorothy met Stan Zbornak as a teenager, and after only one date with him, found out she was pregnant. What Dorothy claimed was a pity date before Stan left for the Korean War turned into marriage, parenthood and her longest relationship.

Dorothy and Stan had two children together, Michael and Kate, but their relationship was never easy, with Stan's many infidelities causing trouble throughout their marriage. Stan and Dorothy eventually moved to Miami, but after 38 years, enough was enough for Dorothy after Stan cheated on her with a much younger woman. They got divorced, and Dorothy moved in with Blanche.

Dorothy is smart, funny and has sophisticated tastes. She enjoys Miami's vibrant performing arts scene and is a talented singer and dancer. Dorothy's sarcastic wit keeps the other housemates in line in the Golden Girls' house, but deep down, Dorothy is a kind and loyal friend to everyone.

Dorothy's bad luck with men continued after her marriage breakdown, and she was often teased by the other girls for being a little desperate. Just when it looked like Dorothy might be alone forever, she meets Blanche's uncle Lucas, and they fall madly in love. Dorothy married Lucas in the final episode, and moved to Hollingsworth Manor in Georgia, near to Blanche's childhood home.

Getting to Know the Girls
Sophia

Sophia Petrillo (née Grisanti) was born in Sicily on 17 April 1906 to Don Angelo and Eleanor Grisanti. Don Angelo and Eleanor had four other children: Angelo, Vito, Regina and Angela.

As a teenager in Sicily, Sophia was briefly engaged to a villager called Augustine Bagatelli, but it didn't work out. After Augustine, she was to marry Giuseppe Mangiacavallo, but he left Sophia at the altar. At the age of fourteen, Sophia moved to the United States after she annulled her arranged marriage to Guido Spirelli. Sophia soon married Salvadore Petrillo, and they had three children, Phil, Gloria and Dorothy, who they brought up in Brooklyn, New York.

While Sophia was a full-time homemaker with no formal education, it is often hinted that she has mafia connections from her life back in Sicily, and perhaps carried out some mob work from time to time.

After her children grew up and moved away, Sophia remained married to Salvadore until he died from a heart attack. After Sophia suffered a stroke that rendered her (in Dorothy's words) 'a complete burden',

she moved into the Shady Pines retirement home in Miami to be near Dorothy. In 1985, a suspicious fire at Shady Pines saw Sophia move in with Dorothy. What was originally a temporary measure turned into a more permanent arrangement.

Sophia's no-nonsense, 'say it how it is' attitude kept the other girls in the house on their toes at all times. While it is suggested that her lack of filter might have had something to do with the stroke she had, it's hard to imagine Sophia ever having been any different. Stories from her youth in Sicily certainly attest to Sophia being one sassy lady for the entirety of her life.

When Dorothy married Lucas Hollingsworth (Blanche's uncle) and moved out of the house, Sophia, Rose and Blanche decided to try their luck in the hotel business, opening the Golden Palace Hotel in Miami. At the end of *The Golden Palace* spin-off series, we see Sophia return to Shady Pines once and for all – with Sophia popping up a few times in another *Golden Girls* spin-off called *Empty Nest*.

May you put your dentures in upside down and chew your head off.

*Please forgive me –
it wasn't my fault.
My cousins have been
marrying each other
for generations.*

Getting to Know the Girls
Rose

Rose Nylund (née Lindström) was born in St Olaf, Minnesota in 1930. Rose was born to a monk named Brother Martin, and Ingrid Kerklavoner, who tragically died giving birth. Rose spent the first years of her life at an orphanage, after being left on the doorstep in a basket with some hickory-smoked cheese. At age eight, Rose was adopted by Gunter and Alma Lindström and, while the Lindströms gave Rose a wonderful home, she still wondered about her birth parents (often fantasising that her father was Bob Hope).

Rose never graduated from high school, thanks to a bout of mono that resulted in her sleeping through the ceremony. Despite this, Rose was still voted 'most likely to get stuck in a tuba' by her graduating class, and went on to study at St. Paul Business School, Rockport Community College, and St. Gustaf University.

Rose met Charlie Nylund in St. Olaf when they were children, but they weren't exactly high school sweethearts – Rose admitted to having 56 boyfriends before they finally tied the knot in 1948. They had five children, Kirsten, Bridget, Gunilla, Adam and Charles Jnr.

Rose and Charlie had a wonderful 32 years of marriage and rumour has it that their sex life was so good that Rose was blissfully unaware of popular television shows like *I Love Lucy*. Sadly, Charlie died in 1980 from a heart attack. He went out with a bang, with Rose telling the girls that he died during a bout of love making. After Charlie's death, Rose decided it was time to leave the memories and inclement weather of St. Olaf behind and make a fresh start in Miami.

Rose is the lovable fool and innocent spirit in the Golden Girls' house, playing the perfect heel to Dorothy and Sophia's acerbic wit and Blanche's over-the-top attitude. Rose loves nothing more than telling a long-winded story about life back in St. Olaf, much to the dismay of her housemates. She is kind, and pure, and is often the butt of Dorothy and Sophia's jokes..

When Dorothy married and moved out of the house, Sophia, Rose and Blanche decided to try their luck and opened the Golden Palace Hotel in Miami. While we never found out what happened to the girls after *The Golden Palace* spin-off was cancelled, I like to think that Rose is living out her days in Miami, perhaps at Shady Pines, spreading kindness and joy and entertaining the other residents with stories about St. Olaf.

Season 1 overview

AIRED: September 1985 — May 1986

BEST EPISODES: The Engagement • That Was No Lady •
Flu Attack • The Way We Met

CLASSIC MOMENT
Stan turning up to breakfast
in Dorothy's robe, much to
the disgust of the other girls.

In Season 1 we are introduced to Blanche, Dorothy, Rose and Sophia. We also meet house chef, Coco, who appears and disappears within the confines of the pilot episode – but not before lending Blanche a supportive ear after her engagement is called off. Well what's a freshly single girl supposed to do but start dating again? Blanche almost gets engaged again later in the season – this time to Richard, a widower with two young children. When Richard gets serious about Blanche and takes the next step, she considers his offer, but realises that her time as a parent of young children is over, and she prefers it that way.

In Season 1 we find out about the girls' former marriages, and what led them to the house in the first place. Dorothy is recently divorced after being married to Stan Zbornak for 38 years. It turns out Stan was a bit of a two-timing *yutz* for most of their relationship, and Dorothy is glad to be rid of him – but that doesn't stop Stan from turning up at her door on a regular basis, first to attend their daughter, Kate's wedding, then again to attempt to rekindle things with Dorothy when his new wife decides to leave him.

We also learn more about Blanche, the confident, sexy and addicted-to-love

homeowner. Blanche's husband George passed away soon after they moved to Miami from Atlanta, leaving her with a broken heart and a big empty house. Despite having a wonderful marriage, Blanche finds solace in her grief by jumping back into dating with gusto. It is established early in the first season that Blanche is the serial dater of the house, although Sophia might call her something a little less flattering (and often to her face!). But Blanche isn't all about dressing up and dating – her sensitive and caring side is also revealed early in the season when she decides to donate a kidney to her sister. Although it turns out that Blanche isn't a suitable blood donor thanks to her incompatible blood vessels, we see for the first time that Blanche is more than just her good looks and flirty out-there attitude.

Season 1 also gives us Rose's back story, who was married to Charlie Nylund for 32 years before he passed away in 1980. Rose and Charlie had a dedicated, happy marriage, and the loss and sadness she experienced after his death led her to her work as a grief counsellor. Season 1 sees Rose re-enter the world of dating for the first time since Charlie died, with hilarious and heart-warming results. In an early episode, Rose strikes up a relationship with a gentleman called Arnie, but is not sure she is ready to take it 'all the way'. She is nervous when they decide to take a cruise together, particularly because the last time she made love, it was with Charlie, and during their love-making session, he died! Spoiler alert – love prevails and they totally get it on anyway. All reports from Rose says it was wonderful. Aww!

And finally, Season 1 introduces us to Sophia, Dorothy's wisecracking mother who moves into the house, temporarily at first, after a fire at Shady Pines retirement home leaves her without a place to stay. While Sophia and Dorothy have a sometimes fiery relationship, their love for each other is shown when Sophia has a health scare and believes she is about to meet her maker. Sophia can't get to the hospital due to a hurricane, so she remains in the house, fearful she is about to have a heart attack. In a touching moment, she admits to Dorothy that she is her favourite daughter. In the end, it turns out that all is okay, and Sophia just has indigestion because of the large meal she ate earlier in the day. Phew!

CLASSIC MOMENT
Blanche being comforted by Coco after being jilted by her fiance, who turned out to be a bigamist.

Episodes

Star Profile

Rue McClanahan

Eddi-Rue McClanahan was born on 21 February 1934 in Healdton, Oklahoma, to Dreda Rheua-Nell (née Medaris) and William Edwin McClanahan. Of Irish and Choctaw heritage, she was raised as a Methodist and graduated from Ardmore High School before earning a Bachelor of Arts degree at the University of Tulsa, majoring in theatre and German.

RUE

McClanahan made her 1957 stage debut in Pennsylvania's Erie Playhouse performance of *Inherit the Wind*, and began acting in Off-Broadway productions that same year. In 1969, twelve years after her theatre debut, she made her Broadway debut playing Sally Weber in the original production of the musical *Jimmy Shine*. McClanahan went on to star in *Father's Day* (1971), *Sticks and Bones* (1972) and *California Suite* (1976).

McClanahan's television career began in 1970 with a role in *Another World* as Caroline Johnson, a woman possessed by love for a man married to someone else, who would go to any lengths to get him (including kidnapping his twin children!). What was initially a guest role soon turned into a recurring character until Caroline was eventually carted off by the authorities. Following her popularity in this role, McClanahan was cast as Margaret Jardin in *Where the Heart Is*.

Like Bea Arthur, McClanahan's breakout hit on television was a role in *Maude*, where she had a six-year tenure between 1972 and 1978 in the role of Vivian Harmon, Maude's sweet-natured neighbour and best friend.

McClanahan's next major television role was as Fran Crowley in *Mama's Family* (1983–1984). Crowley was the journalist sister of 'Mama' Thelma, and in stark contrast to McClanahan's most famous role, she played an uptight snobbish spinster. Coincidentally, Betty White also appeared in the first two seasons of *Mama's Family*, as Thelma's daughter Ellen.

In 1985, McClanahan was cast in *The Golden Girls*, and the legend of Blanche Devereaux was born. She was nominated for four Emmys for the role, winning in 1987 for Outstanding Lead Actress in a Comedy series.

FUN FACT

Between 1958 and 1997, McClanahan was married six times, a tally that would surely intimidate even Blanche Devereaux herself. She even named her 2007 autobiography *My First Five Husbands... and the Ones Who Got Away*.

After the success of *The Golden Girls,* McClanahan went on to star in several made-for-television movies, including the trilogy *Children of the Bride*, *Baby of the Bride* and *Mother of the Bride*.

McClanahan returned to Broadway in 2001 as Countess de Lage in *The Women*, followed by a role as Madame Morrible in the 2005 Broadway production of *Wicked*. McClanahan also acted in various television and movie roles during this period, including as the grandmother in *Blue's Clues* and voice acting work as Scarlett in *Annabelle's Wish*, Anastasia Hardy in *Spider-Man: The Animated Series* and as Bunny in an episode of *King of the Hill*. In 2009 in an episode of *Law & Order* she played a woman who once had an affair with John F. Kennedy – a role befitting the legend of Blanche Devereaux herself!

Outside of television, McClanahan was an active supporter of gay rights and marriage equality in the United States. She was a strict vegetarian and staunch animal rights activist, lending her voice to many animal rights campaigns, including work with PETA (People for the Ethical Treatment of Animals). An active Democrat, McClanahan was a huge supporter of Barack Obama, and once sent an angry letter to John Kerry stating he had lost her vote and respect after it had emerged that he had participated in pheasant hunting.

McClanahan's final acting role was in the TV series *Sordid Lives* in 2008, playing Peggy Ingram. Rue McClanahan died on 3 June 2010 at the age of 76 in New York City. She will be remembered for her warmth and talent, her human rights activism and enduring love of all animals.

I've been allowed to develop my own character, which I'm still working on.

Star Profile

Bea Arthur

Beatrice Arthur was born Bernice Frankel on 13 May 1922 in Brooklyn, New York to Rebecca (née Pressner) and Philip Frankel. In 1933, Arthur's parents moved Bea and her two sisters to Cambridge, Maryland. At age sixteen, she developed coagulopathy, a serious blood disease that resulted in her parents sending her to boarding school in Pennsylvania (presumably because the health care was better there).

BEA

Arthur studied for a year at Blackstone College for Girls in Virginia, before the war effort called and she joined the United States Marine Corps Women's Reserve. Arthur worked as a truck driver and typist during World War II, taking an Honorable Discharge in 1944 as a Staff Sergeant.

A further year of study at Franklin Institute in Philadelphia saw Arthur become a licensed medical technician, but after working in the medical field for a short time, Arthur threw it all away for a shot at fame on the stage in New York City.

In 1947 she enrolled at the Dramatic Workshop of The New School in Manhattan and joined an Off-Broadway theatre group at the Cherry Lane Theatre. Arthur made a great impression early and was consistently in acting work from that point on, spending much of the 1950s and 1960s starring in Broadway and Off-Broadway plays. She was also married twice during this time – firstly to Robert Alan Aurthur (from whom she kept a version of his surname), followed by director Gene Saks in 1950. Arthur also became a mother to two boys during this period, adopting Matthew (born in 1961) and Daniel (born in 1964). Saks and Arthur later divorced in 1978.

Arthur's first taste of big success was the Tony Award she received in 1966 for her portrayal of Vera Charles in the original Broadway production of Jerry Herman's *Mame*. Arthur performed in many other Broadway roles, including as Yente the Matchmaker in *Fiddler on the Roof*, Lucy Brown in *The Threepenny Opera* and as Enid Pollack in *The Floating Light Bulb*.

I'm 5-feet-9, I have a deep voice and I have a way with a line. What can I do about it?

Her first starring role on TV came relatively late in her career – in 1971 Arthur was nearly fifty when she appeared on *All in the Family* as outspoken liberal feminist Maude Findlay. This character was so popular that in 1972 Arthur was offered her own spin-off series, *Maude* – a ground-breaking sitcom that dealt with highly controversial issues at the time, including abortion, drugs and domestic violence. *Maude* ran for six seasons between 1972 and 1978, catapulting Arthur to television stardom in the United States. Her comedic timing and formidable wit later saw her perfectly cast as Dorothy in *The Golden Girls*, where her hilarious one-liners often stole the show.

Outside of Hollywood, Arthur was a card-carrying Democrat who shared many political opinions with her screen characters Maude Findlay and Dorothy Zbornak. She was also a passionate animal rights activist, protesting with PETA (People for the Ethical Treatment of Animals) against the fur trade, foie gras and factory farming. Arthur was also a gay rights campaigner, and shared her wealth with many charities.

Bea Arthur passed away at the age of 86 on 25 April 2009 in Brentwood, Los Angeles. Three days later, the Broadway community paid tribute to her legacy by dimming the marquee lights for one minute at 8 pm.

Arthur will always be remembered for her razor-sharp wit, her classically sardonic delivery of crushing one-liners and for generally being a kick-ass human being who everyone loved. RIP Bea.

FUN FACT

If you want to see Arthur at her sarcastic best, just watch her scathing and hilarious set during Comedy Central's 'Roast of Pamela Anderson'. Arthur and Anderson are both huge supporters of PETA, and it was all in good fun, but this has to be one of the all-time classic roast moments in television history. We would repeat some of the jokes here, but this is a family publication!

Star Profile

Estelle Getty

Estelle Gettleman (née Scher) was born on 25 July 1923, to Sarah and Charles Scher, Polish Jewish immigrants who had moved to New York City and opened a glass store. Getty had two siblings, her sister, Roslyn and brother, David.

ESTELLE

Getty attended Seward Park High School on the Lower East Side of Manhattan, and it was here she first developed an interest in the performing arts. She soon began her career as a comedian and actor with the Yiddish theatre in New York City. She also tried her hand at stand-up comedy in the holiday resorts of the Catskill Mountains, but it seems audiences weren't ready for a female stand-up at the time.

Not one to give up easily, Getty continued to pursue her performing career. A love of Vaudeville drew her to the stage, where she trod the boards Off-Broadway and in community theatres while working a day job as a secretary. Her most notable theatre role was in Harvey Fierstein's *Torch Song Trilogy* during its original Broadway run in 1982.

After making a name for herself on the stage, Getty was a relative unknown when she joined *The Golden Girls* cast. Despite her lack of television experience, she soon won over cast, crew and audiences alike with her comedic style – she had everyone in stitches simply walking across the stage. You wouldn't ever guess it when looking at her incredible performance as Sophia, but Getty suffered terribly from stage fright.

The role of Sophia Petrillo was a huge break for Getty, who had previously only had minor roles. Her son quoted her as wryly saying at the time, 'After fifty years in the business, I'm an overnight success.' Despite playing the role of an octogenarian, Estelle Getty was the second youngest of *The Golden Girls* cast, spending 45 minutes in the makeup chair before each episode to look the part. Between 1986 and 1993, Getty was nominated for seven Emmy awards for Outstanding Supporting Actress in a Comedy Series for *The Golden Girls*, taking out the award in 1988.

FUN FACT

Getty released an exercise video for senior citizens in 1993 entitled *Young at Heart: Body Conditioning*.

After *The Golden Girls*, Getty continued to work in television, with roles in shows including *Empty Nest*, *Blossom* and *Mad About You*. Getty was also a film actor, with roles in movies including *Tootsie*, *Mannequin*, *Mask* and *Stop! Or My Mom Will Shoot*.

Getty often spoke of the fact that she preferred the company of gay men, which led her to be a staunch gay rights supporter and activist. Tragically, Getty's nephew Steve Scher contracted HIV which eventually led to AIDS. Because his parents lived in Britain, Getty took care of him in California until his death in 1991. This was a defining experience for Getty, and she worked in support of several AIDS charities.

Sadly, Getty passed away on 22 July, 2008 in Los Angeles, California, a few days before her 85th birthday. Getty will be remembered for her kind nature and impeccable comedic timing, which gave her universal appeal amongst young and old.

Age does not bring you wisdom, age brings you wrinkles.

Star Profile

Betty White

Betty Marion White Ludden was born on
17 January 1922 in Chicago, Illinois to homemaker
Christine Tess (née Cachikis) and lighting company
executive Horace Logan White. She was an only child,
and her grandparents were of Danish, Greek, English
and Welsh heritage.

Betty White

BETTY

During the Great Depression, White's family moved to California, eventually settling in Los Angeles where she attended Horace Mann School Beverly Hills and Beverly Hills High School. White graduated in 1939, and originally wanted to become a forest ranger, but had to alter her career aspirations after learning that this was a job forbidden to women at the time.

Instead, after developing an early interest in performing, and having written and played the lead in her graduation play at Horace Mann School, she began trying out for a career in show business, getting her start in the performing arts after appearing on radio shows during the early 1940s. But, as it was for many others at the time, her performing career was interrupted by World War II, when she joined the American Women's Voluntary Services.

After the war, White hoped to embark on an acting career, but was turned down by the big studios for not being 'photogenic' enough. A determined White then pursued a career in radio, first reading commercials and playing small parts until getting more work on radio shows like *Blondie*, *The Great Gildersleeve* and *This is Your FBI*. Soon enough, her hard work paid off and she was given her own radio program, *The Betty White Show*.

In 1949, White got her big television break as a co-host on a variety show called *Hollywood on Television*. Throughout the 1950s, she had numerous TV roles, starring in *Life with Elizabeth* and *Date with the Angels,* and her very own variety program *The Betty White Show*. For her role in *Life with Elizabeth*, White was nominated for a Best Actress Emmy in 1951 – the first year ever that a women's Emmy category was awarded (you heard right, folks!).

In the 1960s, White hosted and appeared on dozens of TV game shows. Notable appearances include *Password* and its many spin-offs, *What's My Line?*, *To Tell the Truth*, *I've Got a Secret* and *Pyramid*. By the 1970s she was

FUN FACT

Perennially popular amongst viewers young and old, White holds the record for the longest-spanning television career of any woman, ever!

an established name on radio and on television, but shot to fame in 1973 as the man crazy and sharp-witted Sue Ann Nivens in *The Mary Tyler Moore Show*. For this reason, White was originally cast as Blanche in *The Golden Girls*, while Rue McClanahan read for the role of Rose. After White and McClanahan decided they weren't happy with the original casting, they read for each other's roles during screen testing and the rest is history.

White was still active in game-show land during the early 1980s, winning a Daytime Emmy for Outstanding Game Show Host for her work on *Just Men!* She also had a recurring role on *Mama's Family* in 1983 and 1984, where she worked with *The Golden Girls* co-star Rue McClanahan. In 1985, White was cast in *The Golden Girls* and became one of prime-time television's most beloved stars.

After *The Golden Girls*, White remained active on television with roles in the ill-fated *The Golden Palace*, as well as smaller roles in *Suddenly Susan*, *Yes, Dear* and *The Practice*. The unstoppable White even won the 1996 Emmy for Outstanding Guest Actress in a Comedy Series when she portrayed herself on *The John Larroquette Show*, in an episode that also starred Estelle Getty and Rue McClanahan.

Like her *Golden Girls* contemporaries, White is an animal rights activist who is actively involved in many animal welfare organisations. She has been President Emerita of the Morris Animal Foundation since 2009, and has been on the board of directors of the Greater Los Angeles Zoo Association since 1974. Does this incredible woman ever sleep?

I may be a senior, but so what? I'm still hot.

Season 2 overview

AIRED: September 1986 — May 1987

BEST EPISODES: Isn't it Romantic? •
Vacation • Love, Rose •
'Twas the Nightmare Before Christmas

CLASSIC MOMENT
The girls freak out when Burt Reynolds
comes to the door to take Sophia for
lunch. When he asks 'Which one's the
slut?', they all exclaim: 'I AM!!!'.

In Season 2 we see a focus on the girls trying to make ends meet. In the first episode, we see the girls try to score some extra cash by breeding minks for fur in their garage. Considering most of the actors on *The Golden Girls* were passionate animal rights activists, it was fortunate that the mink business fell through after it turned out the minks were all boys, and in no state for breeding since they preferred the company of the other male minks. In another effort to score some extra cash, we later see Sophia take up a job at Captain Jack's Seafood Shanty, complete with an adorable pirate's uniform, and Rose and Sophia opening a sandwich shop, until they are eventually shut down by the mob.

The girls are also visited by several relatives from out of town during Season 2. Dorothy organises for Sophia's sister Angela (Nancy Walker, 1922–1992) to fly in from Sicily as a surprise, but it turns out they've been estranged for years. In another episode, Rose's daughter Bridget (played by Marilyn Jones) and Dorothy's son Michael (played by Scott Jacoby) visit the house at the same time, and when romance blossoms between them, Dorothy and Rose are absolutely mortified. Later, Dorothy's daughter Kate (Deena Freeman) arrives with news that she's splitting up from her husband because he is cheating. When she decides to go back to him, Dorothy tries to talk her out of it, but it creates a rift between them.

Season 2 sees Blanche confront the passing of time after her pregnancy scare turns out to be menopause. While initially horrified, Blanche is not one to linger on thoughts of ageing for long and keeps her dating game going strong. Blanche even goes on a date with Dorothy's ex-husband Stan as a favour when he turns up one night unannounced and miserable. Dorothy ends up gets jealous when she thinks they have started dating in earnest. But it isn't to be, since it turns out that Stan is yet again dating a much younger woman, and the universe rights itself once more.

In Season 2 we experience a classic Golden Girls love triangle for the first time – really a love quadrilateral, if you crunch the numbers – between Rose, Dorothy, Blanche and Patrick Vaughn (played by Lloyd Bochner, 1924-2005). Patrick is a handsome and mildly famous TV star who turns up in Miami to play the lead role in a local play the girls are also performing in. One by one, the girls realise they are being three-timed by Patrick, culminating in a hilarious confrontation on stage. Dorothy, who is playing the local sheriff in the play, and is of course a woman not to be messed with, reads Patrick the riot act and throws him off the stage and out of town.

In the most heartfelt episode of Season 2, we see the girls planning their Christmas vacations with their families. Sophia and Dorothy are off to New York, Blanche has plans to go back to Georgia and Rose is returning to St. Olaf.

Unfortunately, their plans go awry when they call into the Grief Counselling Center to see Rose and find themselves held up at gunpoint by a disgruntled man dressed as Santa.

But this isn't your standard stick-up looking for cash. Tragically, Santa is holding them up so that he will have people to spend Christmas Day with. Luckily, Sophia saves the day by grabbing his gun and revealing it is just a toy. When the girls finally arrive at the airport, they find that all flights out of Miami have been cancelled. But all is not lost: the girls end up at a local diner and realise that while they will miss their families back home, all they really need is to be together at Christmas – because they are each other's family now.

CLASSIC MOMENT
The girls learning the true meaning of Christmas after being marooned in Miami.

Episodes

I can't pawn this ring! Stan bought it for me. It means so much to me.

He also left you for a 28-year-old stewardess with firm thighs and perky breasts!

You have yourself a ring!

The Golden Girls

Top 10 Episodes of All Time

While we would all love to have the time to watch all seven seasons, from start to finish, over and over again, sometimes it's nice to play the highlights reel. While choosing your favourite *Golden Girls* episode is an almost impossible task, in this author's humble opinion, it is possible to narrow them down to a top ten listing.

These classic episodes are essential viewing for all comedy fans – and will probably convince you to go back and watch the whole series again anyway!

The Engagement
SEASON 1, EPISODE 1

AIRED: 14 September 1985
WRITTEN BY: Susan Harris
DIRECTED BY: Jay Sandrich

A very tight first episode by any standards, and rivalling *Cheers* and *Friends* as the greatest sitcom pilot ever, this storyline established *The Golden Girls* as an overnight success, with viewers hooked from day one.

In this episode, Blanche becomes engaged to Harry (played by Frank Aletter, 1926–2009), a seemingly charming fellow who might just turn out to be too good to be true. After hearing Blanche's engagement news, Dorothy and Rose fear they will have to move out of her house, after only just moving in. They also suspect something is not quite right about Harry, but don't mention it to Blanche.

Meanwhile, Dorothy is busy with another developing crisis: her mother Sophia is suddenly homeless after her retirement home, Shady Pines, burns down under mysterious circumstances. Sophia moves in with the girls while the fire is dealt with, causing tension between Dorothy and Sophia, thanks to Sophia's wisecracking demeanour and tendency to dole out some tough advice (and insults) in her no-nonsense manner.

The episode culminates with Blanche finding out the truth about Harry, when he is arrested moments before their wedding, for – you guessed it – bigamy! Blanche is upset, but the girls are relieved that at least they now know the truth. The episode closes with the girls realising that the bond they have with each other is all that really matters.

FUN FACT
Blanche does not have a
Southern accent in this
episode. Director Jay Sandrich
initially wasn't keen on her
speaking like a Southern belle
in the series, but relented by
the second episode on advice
from the producers.

CLASSIC QUOTE
Sophia: I heard voices,
I thought it was robbers,
so I hid my jewels. Now
I can't remember where.
Dorothy: Ma, you don't
have any jewels!
Sophia: Thank God,
because I can't find them.

Flu Attack

SEASON 1, EPISODE 21

AIRED: 1 March 1986
WRITTEN BY: James Berg,
Stan Zimmerman
DIRECTED BY: Terry Hughes

In an era before the concept of 'man flu' existed, four women alone in a house sharing a head cold set the standard for sick and sorry wallowing. Rose is patient zero, who soon spreads her germs to Blanche and Dorothy; however, Sophia somehow escapes the disease. A doctor is called and they are all instructed to stay at home and rest.

Unfortunately, this news doesn't fit in with the girls' social calendar, with the Volunteer of the Year Awards taking place that weekend and all four girls eligible to win. If this isn't a recipe for tension, simply add some old-fashioned influenza to the mix and stir! Everyone is tired and cranky with each other, and negotiations break down to the point where Blanche, Dorothy and Rose refuse to speak to each other.

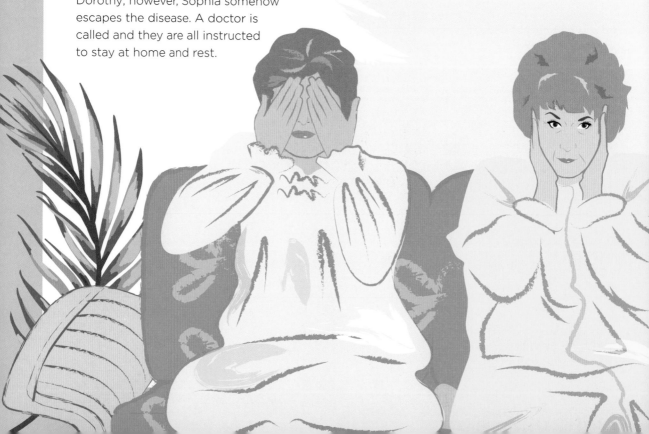

Unencumbered by illness, Sophia makes plans to attend the awards banquet, but cancels the reservations for the other girls, despite suspecting one of them had won. Still deathly ill, the girls attend the banquet anyway, even bringing dates! Not one to be left out of the action, Sophia arrives with Raoul, a much younger man. I won't spoil who wins the award, but rest assured it is one of the Girls.

Of course, a truce is called between the girls and they are all friends again. Phew!

CLASSIC MOMENT

Rose asking if there is any orange juice left, to which Dorothy replies by pouring herself the last of the juice and chugging it as Rose looks on solemnly.

CLASSIC QUOTE

Blanche: Oh, you don't have to worry about me, honey. I never get sick. I take very good care of myself. I treat my body like a temple.
Sophia: Yeah, open to everyone, day or night.

The Way We Met
SEASON 1, EPISODE 25

AIRED: 10 May 1986
WRITTEN BY: Barry Fanaro, Terry Grossman,
Kathy Speer, Winifred Hervey, Mort Nathan
DIRECTED BY: Terry Hughes

Who doesn't love a good old-fashioned
flashback episode? 'The Way We Met' is the
perfect end to the fantastic first season of
The Golden Girls. In this origin story, we are
transported back in time to finally find out
how the girls' household first came to be.

The episode begins with the girls meeting in
the kitchen after watching the movie *Psycho*.
Too freaked out to go to sleep, they get the
cheesecake out and start chatting. They soon
begin to reminisce about how they first met,
with hilarious results.

In the first flashback, we are taken back to
Blanche meeting Rose for the first time at the
local supermarket, in front of the community
notice board. Rose is on the lookout for
a new home after being kicked out of her
apartment because her landlord discovered
her cat. Blanche isn't sure about Rose
because she seems a little too good and
pure, but decides to give her a chance when
she sees Rose give her cat away to a local
boy whose cat had just died.

COMMU

CLASSIC MOMENT

At the end of the episode, when Sophia scares the girls with a kitchen knife — à la Norman Bates.

CLASSIC QUOTE

Rose: I'll make it up to you, Dorothy. I promise. Listen, if there's ever a night where you can't sleep, I'll come to your room and sing 'Kumbaya'.
Dorothy: Rose, I don't know what to say … yes I do … don't ever do that.

CE BOARD

In the second flashback, we see Dorothy arrive at the house for the first time to be interviewed by Blanche as a potential roommate. Sophia is in tow, and her lack of filter combined with her opinions on the house decor and Blanche herself means Dorothy thinks she doesn't stand a chance. Since Blanche has already given Rose a go, she decides to take a chance on Dorothy as well, and the three move in together.

Finally, we are taken back to the supermarket, where we see the girls attempt their first-ever group grocery shop. Tensions rise when it becomes clear that the girls have differing opinions on almost everything. But just when it looks like things won't work out for them after all, Rose tells the first (of many) St. Olaf stories and they all end up in fits of laughter. Rose picks up a cheesecake and they realise everything is going to be alright.

Ladies of the Evening
SEASON 2, EPISODE 2

AIRED: 4 October 1986
WRITTEN BY: Barry Fanaro, Mort Nathan
DIRECTED BY: Terry Hughes

In this hilarious episode, Blanche, Dorothy and Rose are off to a movie premiere starring Burt Reynolds after winning tickets to the exclusive event. The girls decide to stop in for a drink at a hotel bar on their way to the event after Blanche notices a lot of good-looking men around – after all, a lady never misses an opportunity to mingle. Little did the girls know that the men are there for one thing only, and it isn't the piña coladas!

A short time after the girls enter the bar, the police arrive and the jig is up for the bar's many prostitutes. Unfortunately, the girls are caught up in the bust, and are jailed along with the other ladies on the suspicion of prostitution.

In jail, they fear the worst after one of the local ladies attempts to start a fight with Blanche behind bars, but luckily Dorothy steps up to defend her friend and hilarity ensues. Just as it looks like the girls will be spending a night in the cells, Sophia arrives under the guise of bailing them out – only to take the tickets to the premiere for herself.

The episode culminates with one of the all-time classic Golden Girls moments. It's the following day, and the girls are sitting in the lounge recovering from their ordeal. There's a knock at the door, and it's no less than Burt Reynolds, here to pick up Sophia for a lunch date. When Burt asks Sophia 'Which one's the slut?', all three girls put their hands up, exclaiming 'I AM!!' in unison.

FUN FACT
Rue McClanahan's real-life niece (Amelia Kinkade) stars in this episode as one of the prostitutes in prison.

CLASSIC QUOTE
Rose: Sophia, did you come to bail us out?
Dorothy: No, Rose, she's dropping off a manicotti with a file in it.

Isn't It Romantic?

SEASON 2, EPISODE 5

AIRED: 8 November 1986
WRITTEN BY: Jeffrey Duteil
DIRECTED BY: Terry Hughes

This episode sees Dorothy's old friend Jean (played by Lois Nettleton, 1927–2008) visit from out of town. Jean's long-term partner, Pat, has just passed away, so she decides to catch up with Dorothy to get away from it all.

Jean soon becomes fast friends with the other girls, and Rose and Jean begin to spend a lot of time together. Dorothy knows Jean is gay, but suspects Rose doesn't have a clue. This shouldn't be an issue – aside from the fact that Jean is developing feelings for Rose, while Rose remains none the wiser.

One night, Rose and Jean stay up late chatting and talking about the sadness of being widowed. Although Jean is bunking up in Dorothy's room, Rose suggests Jean sleep in her bed so as not to wake up Dorothy. When Jean gets to bed, she decides to be honest with Rose about her feelings. Rose thinks she is talking about friendship at first, but finally has a moment of recognition of what Jean really means. Rose is shocked and pretends to be asleep.

The next day, Rose tells Dorothy what happened. Jean decides to leave early, and Rose stops her so they can talk. Jean apologises and Rose comforts her, saying that she is flattered and Jean has nothing to be sorry about. Rose invites Jean to stay longer and all is well.

The Golden Girls was one of the first prime-time sitcoms to feature a lesbian storyline. In 1987, this episode was nominated for an Emmy award for Outstanding Writing for a Comedy Series, and won the Emmy for Outstanding Directing for a Comedy Series.

CLASSIC MOMENT
Sophia accidentally renting an X-rated movie after the house gets a new VCR machine.

CLASSIC QUOTE
Sophia: For starters, Jean is a lesbian.
Blanche: What's funny about that?
Sophia: You aren't surprised?
Blanche: Of course not. I mean, I've never known any personally, but isn't Danny Thomas one?
Dorothy: Not Lebanese, Blanche, lesbian!

One for the Money
SEASON 3, EPISODE 2

AIRED: 26 September 1987

WRITTEN BY: Kathy Speer, Terry Grossman, Barry Fanaro, Mort Nathan, Winifred Hervey Stallworth

DIRECTED BY: Terry Hughes

This is a flashback episode where the girls reminisce about their many attempts to earn extra money. The conversation kicks off when Sophia gives the girls some water to taste and asks if they would buy it. It turns out to be from the garden hose, but Sophia thinks she's onto a get-rich-quick scheme.

The first flashback is to the girls deciding to start their own wedding catering business, called Miami Moms Catering. The girls are thrilled to land a big job cooking for 300 people. Cut to the next day, and it's 3 am and the girls are still cooking. The bride suddenly turns up at the door to tell them the wedding is off because her fiancé cheated on her. Realising they may be eating chicken for the rest of their lives if the wedding is called off, the girls manage to convince the bride not to dump her man. Just when it looks like their bacon is saved, the bride announces they are eloping to Las Vegas instead and it's chicken on the menu for the foreseeable future in Miami.

In the next flashback, we are transported to Brooklyn in April 1954, when a young Dorothy comes to visit Sophia to ask her to watch the children two days a week so she can take on extra work to save for their first television set. Sophia initially says no, claiming that 'this TV thing is just a fad', but after Dorothy pushes the issue, Sophia admits that she is actually saving for a television for Dorothy's family. Dorothy admits she was actually going to buy one for Sophia – so they agree to stick with the original plan, so that both families can have one.

In the final flashback, we see the girls competing for the $1000 first prize at a dance competition. The girls all try to outdo each other, with hilarious results, but Rose ultimately steals the show with a gravity-defying routine – which, despite Betty White's considerable talent, may have involved the use of a body double on more than one occasion!

FUN FACT
In the flashback scene where Sophia plays her younger self, we see Estelle Getty without her 'ageing' makeup for the first time.

CLASSIC QUOTE
Rose: When I was younger I was known as the Dancing Fool.
Dorothy: How old were you when they dropped the 'dancing' part?

Valentine's Day

SEASON 4, EPISODE 15

AIRED: 11 February 1989
WRITTEN BY: Kathy Speer, Terry Grossman,
Barry Fanaro, Mort Nathan
DIRECTED BY: Terry Hughes

Another flashback episode, but with all new
material, this episode sees the girls stood up
by each of their dates for Valentine's Day.
Essentially a highlights reel of Valentine's
Days past for each girl, this episode begins
with Sophia's flashback to when Sophia and
her husband, Sal, were driving cross-country
to attend a wedding, along with Sophia's
somewhat disapproving father. They have
car troubles in Chicago, and Sal pulls into a
garage. It is Valentine's Day, and Sal surprises
Sophia with a box of chocolates. Moments
later, it's Sal who is in for a surprise after
he stumbles upon a mafia execution while
looking for the bathroom and they all have
to make a run for it. Despite Sophia's claims
to the contrary, the story ends with Dorothy
exclaiming: 'Ma, that never happened – you
were *not* at the St Valentine's massacre!'

The next flashback is to Valentine's Day one
year before, when Rose, Blanche and Dorothy
decided to take a trip to a mountain lodge for
some good old-fashioned rest and relaxation.
When the girls arrive, they are shocked to
discover that the lodge is actually a nudist

camp, and getting naked is compulsory. The girls decide to leave, but are forced to stay for one night because the bus doesn't leave until morning.

Hungry, they sheepishly sneak downstairs wrapped in sheets, but fling them away before walking into the dining room, where they are shocked to discover that everyone is wearing clothes. The maître d' informs them that 'We always dress for dinner here', and 'in your case, we'd appreciate it if you did that for all three meals.'

The final flashback sees Blanche returning to the bar where George proposed, the year after he died. It was their yearly tradition as a couple. A man at the table next to her strikes up a conversation, and it turns out he was thinking about popping the question that night to his date, but is having second thoughts. Blanche coaches him and he decides to go through with it. In a sweet moment, the man's partner arrives, and instead of it being a woman as Blanche had expected, it's actually a man called Victor. Blanche smiles approvingly and we all get the warm and fuzzies for the couple.

CLASSIC MOMENT
When the girls remember buying condoms before their cruise to the Bahamas — and their cover is blown by a highly convoluted price-check announcement.

CLASSIC QUOTE
Blanche: Dorothy, did you ever make love on top of a mountain?
Dorothy: No, the closest I ever came was on top of a fat guy called 'Old Smokey'.

72 Hours
SEASON 5, EPISODE 19

AIRED: 17 February 1990
WRITTEN BY: Tracy Gamble, Richard Vaczy
DIRECTED BY: Terry Hughes

The Golden Girls never shied away from a sensitive topic, and in 1990, there was no more sensitive topic than HIV/AIDS. It was still the early days of the disease in America, and many members of the community remained misinformed and fearful. This episode was one of the first storylines about HIV/AIDS on television and aimed to educate viewers about some of the myths surrounding the disease.

The story begins with Rose getting some frightening news from her doctor. It turns out Rose had received a blood transfusion five years earlier during a gall-bladder removal and is called back to the hospital after it is revealed that a possible contamination has occurred. The girls reassure Rose that she will be okay, but Rose is terrified that if she is HIV positive, she will be ostracised. The girls reassure her and take her to the hospital to get tested, but are shocked to learn that it will take three days to get the results.

There are some great moments in the show that were clearly trying to dispel common misconceptions about the disease. Blanche confides in Rose that she was also tested and understands her fears. Blanche also says it made her think about all the men she had been with, and what precautions she needed to take in the future. Dorothy picks up a pamphlet about how parents need to have conversations with their children about the dangers of HIV. Blanche's line about AIDS not being 'a bad person's disease' or 'God punishing people for their sins' sent a strong message to viewers, and Sophia's initial fear of using the same bathroom as Rose was corrected by Dorothy in a clear lesson about the false rumours being spread about HIV transmission risks.

Thankfully it all works out and Rose gets a clean bill of health, but this episode helped to allay some of the common fears about HIV/AIDS at the time.

CLASSIC MOMENT
Out on the porch when Dorothy talks about how all life is precious, even mosquitoes — before immediately swatting one with her hand.

CLASSIC QUOTE
Rose: Oh, God, this waiting is driving me crazy! Blanche, when you were tested, how did you make it through?
Blanche: Just kept it to myself, and acted like a real bitch to everybody else.
Rose: No wonder we never knew!

Sister of the Bride
SEASON 6, EPISODE 14

AIRED: 12 January 1991
WRITTEN BY: Marc Cherry, Jamie Wooten
DIRECTED BY: Matthew Diamond

This episode sees Blanche's brother Clayton planning to visit Miami with the promise of a surprise announcement. Blanche is thrilled, and expects the surprise to be that Clayton has met a woman. The other girls subtly remind Blanche that Clayton is an out-and-proud gay man, but Blanche is convinced that he was just going through a phase and would get over it.

When Clayton arrives, he announces that he has met someone, and introduces Blanche to his partner, Doug. Blanche is unable to conceal her disappointment, but Clayton is committed to Doug – in fact, he came to tell his sister that he and Doug are soon to be married.

Blanche doesn't take the news well, and seems preoccupied, worried about what others might think. The other girls manage to change Blanche's mind, and in the end she becomes accepting of his brother's union with Doug because Clayton is finally happy.

CLASSIC MOMENT
Dorothy having to physically restrain Sophia from reacting when Clayton suggests that Doug would 'bend over backwards' for him.

CLASSIC QUOTE:
Blanche: I don't really mind Clayton being homosexual, I just don't like him dating men.
Dorothy: You really haven't grasped the concept of this gay thing yet, have you?
Blanche: There must be homosexuals who date women?
Sophia: Yeah, they're called lesbians.

One Flew Out of the Cuckoo's Nest

SEASON 7, EPISODES 25 AND 26

AIRED: 9 May, 1992
WRITTEN BY: Mitchell Hurwitz,
Don Seigel, Jerry Perzigian
DIRECTED BY: Lex Passaris

This is the final episode of *The Golden Girls* (sob!) and a fitting end to a fabulous series. In this two-part episode, Blanche's uncle Lucas (played by Leslie Nielsen, 1926–2010) visits Miami. On the day that Lucas is arriving, Blanche is torn: she has organised a steamy one-night stand with a man she ran into at the produce counter, and so she needs to find someone to dump Uncle Lucas on.

Dorothy reluctantly agrees to take Lucas to dinner at Don's Crab House, but once they arrive they don't have much to talk about, and have some very stilted conversation. Just when Dorothy contemplates leaving, they form a bond once they realise that Blanche has tricked them into spending the evening together by telling each of them how lonely and desperate the other was.

As an act of revenge, they decide to play a practical joke on Blanche that they have fallen in love and are going to get married.

But what starts as a joke soon blossoms into a whirlwind romance, and Dorothy and Lucas do get engaged, but for real this time.

In one of the most heart-warming Golden Girls scenes ever, Dorothy's former husband, Stan, finally makes amends when he 'kidnaps' Dorothy on the way to her wedding by posing as her limo driver. Dorothy thinks Stan is hurt because Dorothy didn't invite him to the wedding, but it turns out he just wanted to give his blessing and show that he cared. After they finally make peace, Dorothy is on her way to the altar again and finally marries Lucas.

Meanwhile, Blanche, Rose and Sophia are deciding what to do after Dorothy leaves the house. Rose plans to move in with her daughter, while Sophia is planning to move with Dorothy and Lucas to his estate in Georgia. But at the last minute, the three girls realise the strength of their friendship, and it occurs to them that they are each other's family now. The girls are going to stay together, and the scene is set for *The Golden Girls* spin-off, *The Golden Palace*.

In the final scene, Dorothy leaves the house after a tearful goodbye, first in a private moment between Dorothy and Sophia, then between all four girls. Don't forget to get the tissues ready for one of television's most emotional (and hilarious) moments of all time.

CLASSIC MOMENT
Blanche totally freaking out during Lucas and Dorothy's pretend proposal, and Dorothy asking Blanche to call her 'Aunt Dorothy'.

CLASSIC QUOTE
Dorothy: Women like me don't grow on trees.
Sophia: Too bad. We could use the shade.

Season 3 overview

AIRED: September 1987 – May 1988

BEST EPISODES: Old Friends • Brotherly Love • Mother's Day

CLASSIC MOMENT
Dorothy grabbing for dollars playing 'Grab That Dough'.

In Season 3, we see Rose inheriting Baby, a prize pig from her uncle in St. Olaf. Rose wants Baby to move into the house, but the other girls initially say no – until they find out that they will inherit $100,000 when Baby dies. After a short time in Miami, Baby appears to be sick, but the veterinarian suggests she simply misses the farm. Reluctantly, the girls send her home to St. Olaf, where Baby (and their potential fortune) dies only a few hours later.

Season 3 is of course peppered with tales of romance for the girls. Sophia finds a spark with Alvin, a friendly man she meets when visiting the boardwalk. Romance is in the air for Dorothy, too, when Stan's brother Ted (played by McLean Stevenson, 1927–1996) turns up to visit. While initially it is Blanche who pursues him after she finds out he's a neurosurgeon, Ted feels threatened by Blanche and ends up going with Dorothy to get a drink instead – and, much to the shock of Stan and Blanche, Dorothy and Ted are discovered making out near the front door the following morning. The romance is short-lived, however. When they go out for dinner Ted reveals that he already has a much younger girlfriend and that Dorothy was simply a one-night stand. Dorothy gets her sweet revenge by announcing

(via the restaurant's microphone) that Ted is impotent. Whatever you do, do not mess with Dorothy Zbornak!

And of course, we haven't heard the last of Dorothy's former husband, Stan, who crosses Dorothy's path again when he finds out that they will both be investigated by the Internal Revenue Service thanks to Stan's haphazard spending habits in the past. Both Stan and Dorothy must pay $2500 each in missed taxes, so Dorothy is forced to sell her diamond ring. When Stan realises how upset Dorothy is, he sells his treasured Corvette to pay their tax bill and buys Dorothy her ring back, proving that he's not such a bad guy after all.

Season 3 sees two big trips out of Miami for the girls. The first occurs when Rose's great-aunt dies in the Bahamas, and she is asked to deliver the eulogy. Unfortunately, this poses a problem for Rose, as she is terrified of public speaking. Blanche and Dorothy decide to support Rose by joining her at the funeral, but Dorothy must face her fear of flying to do so. Even Blanche must face her fears when her recurring nightmare of travelling on a plane full of bald men that crashes into the ocean appears to be coming true when she notices a distinct lack of hair on most of the men in the surrounding seats. Just as the girls are convinced that they are all about to die, the pilot announces that the plane must return to Miami to avoid a tropical storm. Relieved, the girls convince Rose to face her phobia and she successfully delivers her aunt's eulogy to the passengers instead.

In another travel nightmare, the girls travel across the country to Hollywood to star in the game show, *Grab That Dough*. First, they lose their luggage on the flight over, then they find they must sleep in the hotel lobby after their rooms were overbooked, and their purses get stolen. They do eventually make it to the game-show taping, culminating in a hilarious scene where Dorothy and Blanche are pitted against Rose and Sophia. Bea Arthur's performance inside the cash-grabbing tube is a sight to behold.

CLASSIC MOMENT
Sophia developing a special friendship with Alvin.

Episodes

The Golden Crew

A TV Sitcom Dream Team

Some of television's most successful writers and crew worked on *The Golden Girls* during its seven-season run. In fact, all four actors have attributed much of the success of *The Golden Girls* to the talented writers and crew who made the magic happen on set week after week. It's certainly not hard to understand the success of *The Golden Girls* when looking at those who worked on the show.

Paul Junger Witt

From 1983 until his passing in 2018, Paul Junger Witt was married to *The Golden Girls* creator and writer Susan Harris, co-producing with her *The Golden Girls*, *The Golden Palace* and *Empty Nest*. Witt had a long list of directing and producing credits to his name, including *Dead Poets Society*, *Three Kings*, *The John Larroquette Show* and *Soap*, to name a few. His *Dead Poets Society* was nominated for an Academy Award for Best Picture in 1990, losing out to *Driving Miss Daisy* (but we all know that *Field of Dreams* was robbed that year, am I right?).

Susan Harris

An incredibly talented writer and producer, Susan Harris created *The Golden Girls*, along with many other successful television shows, including *Soap*, *Benson*, *It Takes Two*, *Nurses*, *Fay*, *Loves Me, Loves Me Not* and *The Golden Girls* spin-offs *Empty Nest* and *The Golden Palace*. Harris also has an enviable list of writing credits for shows that others created, including *Maude*, *All in the Family*, *The Partridge Family* and *The Good Life*. In 2011 she was inducted into the Television Academy Hall of Fame.

Winifred Hervey

Winifred Hervey is an accomplished writer and producer who produced over 50 episodes of *The Golden Girls*. Harvey started her career writing for *Laverne & Shirley*, *Mork & Mindy*, *Benson* and *The Cosby Show*. She executive-produced *The Fresh Prince of Bel-Air*, *In the House* and *The Steve Harvey Show*, and also wrote many episodes of these programs. Most recently, she was consulting producer and writer of *Half & Half*.

Kathy Speer

A skilled writer and producer, Kathy Speer wrote 19 episodes of *The Golden Girls*, and also produced and co-executive produced over 100 episodes of the show, and for her work was nominated along with her colleagues for two Writers Guild of America awards.

Her work also includes *Benson*, *Hail to the Chief*, *Pacific Station* and *Whoopi*. She also created two original television series, *The Fanelli Boys* and *The Mommies*.

Mitchell Hurwitz

A skilled television producer, writer and actor, Mitchell Hurwitz produced 21 episodes of *The Golden Girls* between 1991 and 1992, and worked as supervising producer on *The Golden Palace*. Hurwitz's biggest accolade is creating the award-winning *Arrested Development*; he also worked as a producer on *Lady Dynamite*, *Flaked*, *Running Wilde*, *Brothers*, *The Ellen Show* and *The John Larroquette Show*. As an actor, his credits include *Portlandia*, *Kroll Show, Community* and *Animals*.

Tony Thomas

Tony Thomas was executive producer for *The Golden Girls*, *Golden Palace* and *Empty Nest*. His other production credits include *Soap*, *Benson*, *It's a Living*, *Beauty and the Beast*, *Lenny*, *Nurses*, *The Office* and *Pearl*. He also co-produced *Dead Poets Society* with fellow *Golden Girls* crew member Paul Junger Witt.

Barry Fanaro

Barry Fanaro is a television and film comedy writer who co-produced many episodes of *The Golden Girls* during its first four seasons. For TV, he produced *The Fanelli Boys*, *Platypus Man* and *The Secret Diary of Desmond Pfeiffer*. Movies he wrote or co-wrote include *Kingpin*, *Men in Black II*, *The Crew* and *I Now Pronounce You Chuck and Larry*.

Marsha Posner Williams

Co-producing 76 episodes of *The Golden Girls*, Marsha Posner Williams has many other production credits to her name, including *Soap*, *Benson*, *Night Court*, *One Big Family* and *Amen*. She was producing *The Golden Girls* during the show's 1986 and 1987 Primetime Emmy wins for Outstanding Comedy Series.

Marc Cherry

A successful writer and producer, Marc Cherry wrote 11 episodes of *The Golden Girls*, and produced 23 episodes of the show. He also wrote and produced for *The Golden Palace*. Cherry's other TV credits include *Desperate Housewives*, *The 5 Mrs. Buchanans* and *Devious Maids*. Cherry was nominated for several Primetime Emmy Awards as part of his work with *Desperate Housewives*.

Christopher Lloyd

Christopher Lloyd is a screenwriter and producer who screen-wrote during the first four seasons of *The Golden Girls*. His other notable works include *Wings*, *Frasier*, *Back to You*, *Out of Practice* and *Modern Family*. Both *Frasier* and *Modern Family* won five consecutive Emmy Awards for Outstanding Comedy Series, with Lloyd being the only person to executive-produce two programs with five-year winning streaks.

Stan Zimmerman

Television writer and producer Stan Zimmerman wrote three early episodes of *The Golden Girls*: 'Flu Attack', 'Adult Education' and 'Blanche and the Younger Man'. Zimmerman has written and produced for several TV shows including *Roseanne*, *Rita Rocks* and *Gilmore Girls*. He wrote the screenplay for *A Very Brady Sequel* and directed two TV movies, *Skirtchasers* in 2016 and *Secs & Execs* in 2017.

Terry Hughes

As well as directing 108 episodes of *The Golden Girls*, Terry Hughes has directed over 70 television shows and telemovies, while also having production roles on many of these. His career highlights include *Friends*, *Whoopi*, *3rd Rock from the Sun* and *Ripping Yarns*, to name only a few. He has won two Primetime Emmy Awards, one in 1987 for Outstanding Directing for a Comedy Series for *The Golden Girls*, and the other in 1985 |for Outstanding Directing for a Variety or Music Program for *Sweeney Todd: The Demon Barber of Fleet Street*.

Judy Evans

All hail Judy Evans, the masterful costume designer for every episode of *The Golden Girls*! Evans had a long career working on many other television shows including *The Golden Girls* spin-off *Empty Nest*, *Herman's Head*, *Beauty and the Beast*, *Benson* and *Soap*. Her incredible designs and illustrations led her to receive several awards during her life, including winning the Primetime Emmy in 1989 for Outstanding Costume Design for a Series with *Beauty and the Beast*. She was nominated for the same award in 1986 for *The Golden Girls* but lost out to Al Lehman, who designed for *Murder, She Wrote*.

Shady Pines is the retirement home that Sophia resided in until a suspicious fire occurred, forcing Sophia to move in with Dorothy. Throughout the show, Dorothy uses Shady Pines as a thinly veiled threat to keep Sophia in line – uttering 'Shady Pines, Ma!' every time Sophia acts out. Sophia hated Shady Pines, but does return periodically to catch up with friends and generally get herself into trouble.

In the final season, we finally get to meet one of the Shady Pines staff when Sophia breaks both of her ankles and has to use a wheelchair as she recovers. Needing some extra help, Dorothy hires a nurse, who Sophia is horrified to discover is Nurse DeFarge from Shady Pines (played by Edie McClurg, famous for her role as Grace in *Ferris Bueller's Day Off*).

While Sophia is initially suspicious of DeFarge, they soon bond over the nurse's salty demeanour towards the other girls in the house. When it looks like Dorothy and Rose are about to fire DeFarge, Sophia fakes a leg cramp to ensure she has to stay. The girls finally get rid of nurse DeFarge when Sophia is caught out of her chair and dancing around the living room. So it was goodbye to DeFarge and hello to an upwardly mobile Sophia.

In *The Golden Girls* spin-off *The Golden Palace*, we finally get to visit Shady Pines during the double episode when Dorothy visits Sophia and the girls at the Golden Palace. Dorothy is concerned that her mother is working too hard at the hotel, and tries to convince Sophia to move in with her and Lucas at their home in Georgia instead. To avoid having to choose between staying with Blanche and Rose, or moving in with Dorothy, Sophia runs away to Shady Pines. While there, Sophia discovers that things have improved significantly since she last lived there and Shady Pines is not so bad after all.

When Dorothy finally finds Sophia, Sophia tells Dorothy that while Shady Pines would be a nice place to live, the retirement home makes her feel old, but working at the Golden Palace with Rose and Blanche makes her feel useful and happy. Dorothy accepts Sophia's wishes, and tells the girls how proud she is of all of them for making the hotel a success.

FUN FACT
A relatively unknown Jack Black stars in this episode of *The Golden Palace* as the cab driver who takes Sophia to Shady Pines.

Season 4 overview

AIRED: October 1988 — May 1989

BEST EPISODES: Yes, We Have No Havanas •
Valentine's Day • High Anxiety

KNISH
BAR

CLASSIC MOMENT
The girls working hard at Sophia
and Max's ill-fated Knish Bar.

Season 4 begins with a love triangle between Sophia, Blanche and Fidel Santiago (Henry Darrow), an elderly man in the cigar business. While dating two women seems like a dream come true, it turns out to be too much to handle for Fidel, and he dies suddenly. When the girls attend his funeral, Sophia and Blanche mend their feud after they realise that Fidel was practically dating every woman in Miami.

In Episode 5, Blanche and Rose star in a local production of *Cats*, and their smoking-hot cat costumes are a sight to behold. In the same episode, Stan turns up under the guise of taking Sophia and Dorothy to a baseball game. Dorothy and Sophia are right to be suspicious – it turns out Stan is bankrupt, and he is buttering them up in order to borrow money. Just as Dorothy announces they are leaving, Sophia is suddenly hit in the head by a baseball. Ever the opportunist, Stan decides to sue the ballpark to make a quick buck. But like all of Stan's get-rich-quick schemes, it falls apart and Stan leaves empty handed. We don't hear from Stan again, until he returns later in the series to try and recruit the girls into a personal development guru's pyramid scheme, a plan fit for Stan if we've ever heard one.

Season 4 sees Sophia find love with Max Weinstock (played by Jack Gilford, 1908–1990), the ex-business partner of Sophia's late husband Salvadore, who she makes peace with at his wife, Esther's funeral, after their long feud. Max and Sophia fall in love and things move very fast when they decide to tie the knot after only a few days of being together. They decide to open a pizza knish stand in Miami, just like their families had done back in Brooklyn, but business isn't great, and neither is their romance. Although they officially break up, they actually remain married because Sophia is a good Catholic and doesn't believe in divorce.

Later, the girls become diet-obsessed after they're invited to a pool party and they all realise they have gained a few pounds. Meanwhile, after weighing 99 pounds for fifty years, Sophia discovers she now weighs 98 pounds, and panics at the news of her weight loss. All of this diet talk makes the girls reminisce about former health kicks they've been on, including the time that the girls took up aerobics and were pressured into buying super-expensive, over-the-top new outfits, with hilarious results.

To round out Season 4, Sophia almost sells the house from underneath Blanche when a

'For Sale' sign is mistakenly placed in the girls' front yard. While Blanche is initially horrified, she changes her mind when she sees what someone is willing to offer for the house and considers taking the offer. As the girls start making plans to go their separate ways, the buyer pulls out at the last minute and their future in the house is secured once again.

Perhaps the strangest storyline of the season is in Episode 3, when Rose is convinced that aliens visit the house. Dorothy tries to talk sense to her, but Rose is convinced. The episode ends with what we presume are actual aliens flying by the lanai, but don't take my word for it – you be the judge!

CLASSIC MOMENT
Sophia walking down the aisle with Max Weinstock.

Episodes

The Fifth Golden Girl
Coco

Let me take you on a journey. A journey back to a long, long time ago, when New Coke replaced original Coke, compact discs were released for the first time ... and there were *five* roommates in *The Golden Girls* house instead of four.

Originally, Coco was to be one of *The Golden Girls* main characters, as the girls' live-in chef and all-round house boy. An openly gay man, Coco – played by Charles Levin – was quite a natural fit for the house and gave the girls a run for their money in the wit and hilarity stakes ... but alas, it was not to be. After shooting Episode 1, it was decided that five main characters were just too many.

Even a hard-core fan of *The Golden Girls* could be excused for Coco's blink-and-you'll-miss-it role during the series pilot. In the first episode, Coco can be seen tending to meals in the kitchen and comforting Blanche after her shock break-up with her fiancé, but his appearance in the house is never really explained.

Although Levin's performance was great and Coco was well liked by test audiences, it was clear there were just too many central characters. Someone had to be voted off the island, and unfortunately for Levin, Coco was no more. Interestingly, the character of Sophia was supposed to be a guest-starring role only, which could have made room for Coco, but she was so popular with early test audiences she needed a starring role. What was good for Sophia was bad news for Coco: there was just too much going on to keep his storyline in.

Most of Coco's scenes from the first episode were cut so his disappearance from later episodes would be less obvious. While Levin loved working with the girls and was disappointed, he certainly wasn't out of work for very long. Levin can be seen in many 80s and 90s sitcoms and dramas, including *Growing Pains*, *NYPD Blue*, *Murphy Brown*, *Designing Women*, *Seinfeld*, *L.A. Law*, *Doogie Howser, M.D.*, *Night Court* and *Punky Brewster*. Although Coco's role was cut short, Levin did appear in one episode of *The Golden Girls* spin-off *Empty Nest* – but not as Coco.

Coco, we hardly knew ye, but you will always be remembered in Golden Girls folklore as the fifth Golden Girl that never was.

FUN FACT
In the Greek television version of *The Golden Girls*, Coco remains a main character, and shares bunk beds with the character based on Sophia!

The Golden Girls
Cameos

Like any good sitcom worth its salt, *The Golden Girls* had a long line of great actors arriving to stir things up over all seven seasons. Many notable actors walked through the front door of the Golden Girls' house over the years, with a mix of established thespians and fresh-faced unknowns who would reach stardom at a later date.

Here is a collection of the most notable guest stars to make the acquaintances of Blanche, Dorothy, Rose and Sophia.

Mario Lopez

Lopez starred in 'Dorothy's Prized Pupil' (S02E21) where he played Mario, a student of Dorothy's who writes a prize-winning essay on being an American. When the authorities find out that Mario is in America illegally, he is deported and Dorothy is devastated.

Two years after shooting *The Golden Girls*, Lopez scored his most famous role to date: as cool kid and dreamboat extraordinaire A.C. Slater in *Saved by the Bell*. Since that series franchise wrapped up in 1994, Lopez has had roles in *Pacific Blue*, *The Bold and the Beautiful*, *Nip/Tuck* and *Nashville*. Watch out for him playing himself amongst several other famous cameos in the movie *Pauly Shore is Dead*.

Jenny Lewis

Lewis starred in 'Old Friends' (S03E01) where she played Daisy, one of Rose's 'Sunshine Cadets' (think Girl Scouts), who holds Rose's treasured teddy bear hostage (you heard me). Sure, the gun was a water pistol filled with red dye, but we were all deeply concerned for the fate of Fernando the bear. Rest assured, the bear is safe after Rose takes the opportunity to snatch the bear away at the last moment after delivering a very convincing forgiveness speech.

While Jenny Lewis is now an established musician, she has had numerous acting roles since she was a child, including *Troop Beverly Hills*, *Roseanne*, *Baywatch*, *Brooklyn Bridge*, *Pleasantville* and *American Dad!* Be sure to check out the hilarious film clip to Lewis' song 'She's Not Me', where she reprises her role on *The Golden Girls*, and is joined by Fred Armisen as Sophia, Vanessa Bayer as Rose and Zosia Mamet as Dorothy.

George Clooney

Clooney appears in 'To Catch a Neighbor' (S02E24), where he plays police officer Bobby Hopkins. Bobby and fellow police officer Al Mullins (played by Joe Campanella, 1924–2018) run a stake-out at the girls' house to investigate the suspected jewel thieves next door. Bobby ends up getting shot during a sting operation, but the girls comfort him in hospital and all is good in the world again.

Clooney went on to play Booker Brooks in a recurring role on *Roseanne*, which led to his casting as heart-throb Doctor Doug Ross in *ER* – a role that shot him into absolute superstardom. Clooney hasn't had a day out of work since.

From Dusk till Dawn, *Batman & Robin*, *Three Kings*, *O Brother, Where Art Thou?* and *Ocean's Eleven* are just a few of Clooney's movie roles to date. His award highlights include winning an Academy Award for Best Actor in a Supporting Role for *Syriana* in 2005 and multiple Golden Globes nominations and wins.

Quentin Tarantino

Tarantino played an Elvis impersonator at the wedding of Sophia and Max in 'Sophia's Wedding: Part 1' (S04E06). His 1988 appearance was so tiny that he is actually the lowest-billed Elvis impersonator on IMDb for this role.

Tarantino went on to become a movie-making powerhouse, with many successful movies including *Reservoir Dogs, Pulp Fiction, Natural Born Killers, From Dusk till Dawn, Kill Bill, Inglourious Basterds* and *Django Unchained*. This guy gets around: he even played Kermit's director in *The Muppets' Wizard of Oz*.

After they were famous

Burt Reynolds

Burt Reynolds (1936–2018) guest stars in the hilarious episode *Ladies of the Evening* (S02E02), where the girls win tickets to attend the premiere party for a Burt Reynolds film, but end up in jail instead (don't you hate when that happens?).

Reynolds was a huge TV and movie star at the time, having appeared in hit movies including *Deliverance, Smokey and the Bandit, The Cannonball Run* and *The Best Little Whorehouse in Texas*. His 1972 naked centrefold in *Cosmopolitan* magazine solidified his reputation as a Hollywood heart-throb, but despite his fame, Reynolds was reportedly still quite nervous about his scene in *The Golden Girls*. After his appearance on the show, he went on to have his own successful sitcom called *Evening Shade*, which ran for four seasons between 1990 and 1994.

Mickey Rooney

Mickey Rooney (1920–2014) appears in 'Larceny and Old Lace' (S03E21) as Sophia's boyfriend Rocco, who Sophia believes to be an ex-gangster who has robbed a bank just to woo her. When Sophia realises that the gangster act is in fact a ruse and Rocco is just a lonely man with his life savings in his man-bag, the jig is up and they are through.

Mickey Rooney was one of the biggest movie stars ever, getting his start in vaudeville as a child and landing his first movie role at the tender age of six. During the 1930s and 1940s, Rooney starred as the protagonist in the Andy Hardy movies released by MGM, making him one of the most bankable young actors of his generation. Rooney went on to star in hundreds of films, with notable works including *A Midsummer Night's Dream*, *Boys Town*, *National Velvet* and *Breakfast at Tiffany's*. Rooney also gave Rue McClanahan a run for her money in the marriage stakes – walking down the aisle no less than eight times.

Leslie Nielsen

Leslie Nielsen (1926–2010) played Lucas Hollingsworth, Blanche's uncle and Dorothy's eventual husband. Perfectly cast as a love match to the witty and hilarious Dorothy, Nielsen might be the only man we might be able to forgive for stealing her away from our screens during the final episode when they marry and move to his mansion in Georgia.

Nielsen had a long and distinguished acting career. Most of us know him from his comedic roles, first in the *Police Squad!* television series, followed by *Airplane!* (also known as *Flying High*) and the iconic *Naked Gun* movies. But Nielsen also had a serious side, with dramatic roles in *Forbidden Planet* and *The Poseidon Adventure* bringing him fame before his comedic career took off.

Debbie Reynolds

Debbie Reynolds (1932–2016) played Truby, a potential new roommate interviewed by Blanche after Dorothy rekindles her romance with Stan and it looks like she might move out of the house. Naturally, Stan ruins everything by suggesting that Dorothy sign a pre-nup, so the wedding is off and Truby misses out on moving in.

Reynolds is probably best known to the millennial generation from of her role as Grace Adler's mother Bobbi in hit TV sitcom *Will & Grace*, but Reynolds was a huge star for nearly seven decades, with singing and acting talent in spades. Her 1952 breakout lead role in *Singin' in the Rain* made her an overnight sensation, and she went on to star in dozens of film and stage roles over her very long career. Reynolds is also the mother of Princess Leia herself, the late and great Carrie Fisher (1956–2016).

Alex Trebek

Trebek stars as himself in 'Questions and Answers' (S07E17), the episode that sees Dorothy have a dream sequence where she plays against Rose and her neighbour Charlie in a bizarre episode of *Jeopardy!*

Canadian-born Trebek has been hosting shows on Canadian and American television since 1963, and since 1984 has been at the helm of the incredibly popular game show *Jeopardy!* (just ask my mother, the world's biggest *Jeopardy!* fangirl). In 2014, he received a Guinness World Records award for hosting the most-ever episodes of a game show, with a record of 6829 episodes for *Jeopardy!*.

Dating Gold
The Top 10 Exes

The Golden Girls proved once and for all that life can start after 50, with romance most definitely included. While all four girls enjoyed long marriages before moving in together, they also had their fair share of romance as single women.

While we all remember Blanche as the serial-dating sex kitten of the house, the other girls certainly got plenty of the dating action, too. Since listing every ex-boyfriend could fill a book in itself, here is the definitive list of *The Golden Girls* ten most notable exes.

Miles Webber

Miles Webber (played by Harold Gould, 1923–2010) is a college professor who dated Rose over a number of years, and appeared in 13 episodes of *The Golden Girls*. Rose meets Miles at a dance class and they soon start dating. While Miles appears to be all charm, he slips up big time when he makes a pass at Dorothy on the lanai during Blanche's 'Moonlight Madness' party, and we never quite forgave him for it.

To make things worse, Rose finds out that Miles is actually Nicholas Carbone, a man in witness protection who moved to Miami after ratting out a mob boss in Chicago. Rose is distraught after Miles tells her they can only be together if she enters witness protection as well. She reluctantly decides to move with Miles to Chicago; however, it doesn't pan out, so Rose stays in Miami with the girls.

Miles/Nicholas does return to Miami a few months later, only to discover that Rose is now dating a man called Karl. Much to his horror, Karl is actually the mobster who was after Miles! But it all works out after Karl is arrested, leaving Miles free to stay in Miami again. He and Rose continue to date and even consider getting married, but ultimately don't go through with it.

Miles first shows up in Season 5 – but if he seems familiar, that's because Harold Gould also appears in Season 1, in the episode 'Rose the Prude', as Arnie Peterson, the first man Rose slept with after Charlie passed away.

Toshiro Mitsumo

Toshiro Mitsumo (played by Keye Luke, 1904–1991) is a gardener tasked with taking care of the girls' garden. Sophia takes a shine to Toshiro, and attempts to invite him in for a lemonade, but there is a clear language barrier. This doesn't stop Sophia, who manages to invite him over for dinner. He brings over some sushi, which Sophia isn't really into, but it turns out she is totally into Toshiro, and they share a romantic moment together.

Sophia returns the dinner favour by cooking Toshiro her famous spaghetti marinara, followed by her *pièce de résistance*: veal piccata. In a totally adorable moment, they share their first kiss … THEN WE NEVER SEE OR HEAR OF TOSHIRO AGAIN BECAUSE LOVE ISN'T REAL.

Stan Zbornak

Stan Zbornak (played by Herb Edelman, 1933–1996) is the novelty salesman and 'yellow-bellied sleazeball' that Dorothy was married to for 38 years. Stan and Dorothy's relationship began after a one-night stand in the back of Stan's Chevy at a drive-in movie, which resulted in Dorothy becoming pregnant. Stan was unfaithful several times during their marriage, and his affair with flight attendant Chrissy results in their divorce.

Stan is a recurring character throughout the entire series, often returning to Dorothy's life at the most inconvenient times. In moments of weakness, Dorothy had a few flings with Stan after their divorce, and much to Sophia's disgust, nearly married him for a second time. Luckily Stan's insistence on a pre-nuptial agreement made Dorothy realise she didn't want to make the same mistake twice. Why the pre-nup, you ask? Stan had struck it rich after inventing the Zbornie, a baked-potato opener ... because of course he did.

Don, the Beatles impersonator

One of Dorothy's biggest regrets was missing a Beatles concert at the Shea Stadium when one of her children had the flu – so she is thrilled when she wins tickets to a *Beatlemania* dinner theatre show and meets Don (played by Terry Kiser), who plays George Harrison in the tribute band.

The next morning, the girls are shocked to discover that Dorothy has a man in the house, and he is wearing one of her robes. Don and Dorothy have a whirlwind romance, until Dorothy convinces Don to give up the tribute band and go solo. But there's just one problem: his solo show is atrocious. Horrified, Dorothy sneaks out before the performance ends – and just like that, it's all over between them.

Don does try his luck one more time, but this time with Rose, after he turns up at the door with news that he's playing the role of Paul McCartney that week instead. She takes him up on his offer of coffee, because who could say no to Macca?

Sonny Bono & Lyle Waggoner

Dorothy finds herself caught in a love triangle with two celebrities: none other than Sonny Bono (1935–1998) and Lyle Waggoner. It all started after Dorothy went to a dinner theatre to see Sonny and Lyle star in a production of *Equus*. In Dorothy's own words, 'Our six eyes met' and it was true love.

Dorothy is torn about who to keep dating. The girls run into Lyle at a restaurant, but despite Lyle working the room and loudly dropping his own name at every opportunity, Dorothy lets him down gently because she has decided to go on a date with Sonny Bono that night instead.

Sonny turns up to the house to see Dorothy, and Sophia is thrilled – but Dorothy all of a sudden isn't into it and goes back to dating Lyle. In a last-ditch effort to win Dorothy's heart, Sonny uses his power as Mayor of Palm Springs to have Waggoner falsely arrested.

Just when it looks like Dorothy has found true love with Sonny, we find out that it was all just a sub-plot of Blanche's dream about her late husband, George, still being alive, and none of this actually happened.

Max Weinstock

Max Weinstock (played by Jack Gilford, 1908–1990) was Sophia's late husband Salvadore's ex-business partner. Their business partnership ended in 1949 under unfortunate circumstances and Sophia always blamed Max for destroying the family business.

Dorothy and Sophia attend the funeral of Max's wife, Esther, in Brooklyn, and Sophia tells Max off for destroying everything. But Max drops a truth bomb – it turns out it was Sal's fault after all, because he gambled the profits on a horse that never came in.

Sophia and Max finally make peace, and then, you guessed it – romance blooms and they fall in love. Before we know it, Max and Sophia are walking down the aisle. Soon enough, the romance fizzles out, but Sophia and Max remain friends. In fact, they never actually get divorced due to Sophia's Catholic beliefs.

Ken Whittingham

Dorothy's lawyer boyfriend, Ken Whittingham (played by Dick Van Dyke) seems too good to be true: handsome, wealthy and kind enough to dress up as a clown and visit sick children in his spare time. Just when everything is going well and Dorothy expects him to pop the big question, Ken instead surprises Dorothy with the admission that he is quitting the law to become a full-time circus clown.

Dorothy sees this as a threat to their relationship – and quite frankly, can't cope with the clowning. She realises she doesn't really love him and decides to end it.

Dorothy and Ken's break-up scene is one of the funniest *Golden Girls* moments ever. As Dorothy says her tearful goodbye speech, Ken offers her a handkerchief, which of course turns out to be a long colourful array of handkerchiefs strung together that she solemnly drags from the room.

Dr Jonathan Newman

Rose meets Dr Jonathan Newman (played by Brent Collins, 1941–1988) at the grief centre where he works as a psychologist. Rose is really into Jonathan and the girls are keen to meet him, but Rose hesitates. It turns out that Jonathan is a man of short stature, and Rose is worried the other girls will make fun of her.

Blanche goes behind Rose's back and invites Jonathan to dinner. Rose is annoyed, but goes along with it. Cue every bad joke about little people in the book. When Jonathan turns up, Blanche mistakes him for a child ('No thank you, little boy, we already take the *Miami Herald'*) and Blanche accuses Rose of playing a prank on her.

Naturally, shrimp and short ribs are on the menu for dinner. Yes, the dialogue is extremely awkward, and yes, this was another time. Thankfully, the girls learn a lesson about treating people differently after they all have a frank conversation with Jonathan, who is infinitely patient with them.

Unfortunately, things don't work out between Rose and Jonathan after he tells her he can't date her anymore because he couldn't possibly end up with someone who isn't Jewish.

Alvin Newcastle

One day while visiting the boardwalk, Sophia meets Alvin Newcastle (played by Joe Seneca, 1919–1996) and they strike up a conversation. Alvin shows her his security guard ID, saying he works at a local retirement home.

Sophia offers him half of her veal and pepper sandwich, and of course, who wouldn't fall in love with that? They entertain themselves by spotting swimmers peeing in the ocean. Sophia asks Alvin about his late wife, but he avoids answering. At first she thinks he is being rude, but then he gets upset and starts to cry. Sophia comforts him, but she can't work out what is wrong.

The next day, Sophia meets him at the boardwalk again and Alvin doesn't remember her at all. Alvin's daughter tells Dorothy that Alvin has Alzheimer's disease, which explains his forgetfulness. Dorothy tells Sophia that he is sick, but Sophia stands by her man. Alvin eventually moves to New York for better medical care, but Sophia will always remember him.

Thor Anderson

One day, Rose receives a phone call from one Thor Anderson (played by Ken Berry, 1933–2018), a St. Olaf man who remembers her from their youth. He wants to visit Miami and catch up on old times, but there's a problem: Rose has no idea who he is.

When Thor arrives, Rose and Blanche try to find out more about him in order to jog Rose's memory. Eventually, Rose remembers – she briefly dated Thor after she and Charlie broke up for a short time, but it was only to make Charlie jealous. Worse still, she remembers something far more sinister: Thor was a terrible kisser!

Just when it seems things couldn't get worse, it turns out that Thor has been saving for nine years for a bus ticket from St. Olaf to Miami just to tell Rose how he feels. When he admits his undying love for her, Rose doesn't know what to do, but Thor gets the impression that they are going to end up together.

Rose eventually confesses that she does not remember him, and lets him down gently before he leaves town, but not after one last kiss. You guessed it – 40 years later and Thor is still a terrible kisser!

Well, what do you know?
Sophia has a past!

That's right!
But unlike yours, I didn't
need penicillin to get
through it.

Season 5 overview

AIRED: September 1989 — May 1990

BEST EPISODES: Love Under the Big Top •
Have Yourself a Very Little Christmas • 72 Hours

Season 5 of *The Golden Girls* explores some dark themes amongst the usual hilarity. Rose has a close call when she faces the prospect of having HIV after finding out that she received a contaminated blood transfusion during her gall bladder procedure. Dorothy has her own health scare with her battle to be taken seriously when she fights to get a diagnosis for her chronic fatigue syndrome. Sophia decides to help a friend commit suicide, but manages to convince her at the last minute that life is worth living.

There is sad news for Blanche when Big Daddy passes away in Atlanta. Blanche feels terrible guilt for not visiting the last time Big Daddy asked her to, choosing to attend a pageant instead. When Blanche returns home for his funeral, she has an argument with her sister Virginia, who is angry at Blanche for being selfish. Poor Blanche must cope with the guilt of missing her chance to say goodbye to Big Daddy, and realising that with both her parents gone, she is no longer anyone's little girl.

Later, there is further shocking news for Blanche when she finds out that her husband, George, had a secret son called David. Blanche initially rejects David and never wants to see him again, but Rose convinces Blanche to be kind |to him after revealing that her husband, Charlie, had also cheated on her once, but Rose found it in her heart to forgive him for his mistake, so Blanche should too.

Despite featuring some serious themes, there are still plenty of laughs to be had during Season 5. After a friend from high school dies, Dorothy decides it is time to start living. In an effort to complete the bucket list she finds in an old yearbook, Dorothy decides to attempt stand-up comedy at a local nightclub. Despite Sophia's hilarious attempts at crowd participation, Dorothy's performance initially falls flat, however she starts to get big laughs when she starts making fun of herself and her life as a divorced substitute teacher forced to date older men.

CLASSIC MOMENT

Dorothy and Sophia dressed as Sonny and Cher for the Shady Pines mother/daughter beauty pageant.

The hilarity doesn't stop there in Season 5. In one of the funniest ever *Golden Girls* moments, Dorothy and Sophia enter the Shady Pines mother/daughter beauty pageant in order for Sophia to finally beat her old nemesis Gladys Goldfein. Going the extra mile, they decide to dress as Sonny and Cher for the talent section. Sophia and Dorothy's hilarious lounge-room rehearsal of their performance includes a rendition of 'I Got You Babe', complete with Dorothy perfecting Cher's trademark hair flick. Although Sophia and Dorothy are only runners-up in the contest, they take solace in the fact that they *did* beat Gladys Goldfein.

Season 5 includes the beginning of a big romantic storyline for Rose, when she meets college professor Miles Webber for the first time. There is also romance for Dorothy, who finds love with Ken Whittingham, a successful lawyer with a complicated hobby: dressing as a clown and visiting sick children in hospital. While this is initially charming to Dorothy, she is concerned when he decides to quit the law to be a full-time clown. They eventually break up over his decision, but this episode is filled with hilarious moments, including Ken offering her a hanky when they break up, and Dorothy walking off with a stream of colourful clown hankies trailing from his pocket.

As per usual, Blanche gets her share of romance in Season 5 too, but all doesn't go to plan. Things are getting serious with her new boyfriend, Steven, but she has second thoughts after he suffers a heart attack, and avoids visiting him in hospital. Blanche is trying to protect herself because she cares for Steven a lot, and is afraid he might die and leave her like her late husband, George. After Blanche changes her mind and turns up to the hospital to apologise, Steven tells her that he has rekindled his romance with his ex because she was there for him when Blanche wasn't. Luckily for Blanche, she soon cheers herself up by dating the man in the adjacent hospital bed!

Episodes

Hometown Girls
Rose in St. Olaf

St. Olaf is the quirky small town in Minnesota where Rose grew up and spent her life before moving to Miami. Although located in the States, St. Olaf was strongly influenced by Norwegian culture, with most townsfolk being bilingual.

St. Olaf's biggest claim to fame is its giant black hole, where townspeople could be found on weekends 'just standing around looking at it'. Well what else is there to do in St. Olaf? It turns out, the answer is plenty. You could enjoy one of the town's many festivals, like Hay Day (when all the townsfolk celebrate hay), 'The Crowning of the Princess Pig' (I'm guessing a pig is crowned), 'The Festival of the Dancing Sturgeons' (where locals watch sturgeon fish flopping around on the dock), 'The Day of the Wheat' (where people dress up as sandwiches), the 'Butter Queen' competition (which Rose almost won one year, except her butter churn jammed), and of course a milk-diving competition (in which Rose once proudly ranked in the 'low fat' division).

During World War II, St. Olaf's high school was taken over by Nazis, to teach propaganda to the local youth in preparation for a German invasion of America. According to Rose, Adolf Hitler taught history at the school, with Eva Braun instructing students in physical education.

Even though Rose tells many stories about life in St. Olaf, we only get a glimpse of the town on three occasions during *The Golden Girls*. In 'Yokel Hero' (S04E04), the girls finally visit St. Olaf after Rose is nominated for St. Olaf's Woman of the Year Award. Naturally, Rose took home first prize – a golden trophy made of chocolate and wrapped in foil.

FUN FACT
There is a statue of Blanche Devereaux in St. Olaf! The townspeople erected the tribute in recognition of Blanche returning to them a surplus of war bonds she found in a box of junk she'd bought off Rose.

Hometown Girls
Sophia in Sicily

When it's time to return to Sicily, three different suitors beg her to stay. But she can't decide who to choose, so she chooses none of them. But she agrees to meet with them at the same resort many years later. To her trio of suitors, that eventful gathering was referred to as 'Rendezvous with Sophia'. But to the rest of the world, it was better known as the Yalta Conference ...

Picture it: Sicily, 1906. A beautiful baby girl is born by the name of Sophia Grisanti, and when she grows up, nobody will be safe from her wisecracks and insults.

Sophia lived in Sicily until emigrating to the US at age 14. Her life in Sicily was that of a traditional Roman Catholic living in a small village: good food and drink, fresh country air and a smattering of traditional Sicilian curses. Sophia continually alludes to the mafia undercurrent back in Italy, and in Sophia's own words, Sicily's main export back then was ransom notes. While still very young, it appears that Sophia had some involvement in mafia work back in the motherland, and she once bragged that no one in her family had 'ever left a body to be found'.

Sicily was also a place of grand romance for Sophia, with many notable trysts involving Pablo Picasso, Sigmund Freud and Winston Churchill, to name a few. It was also the place where she met her true love and husband, Salvadore Petrillo.

While many of Sophia's stories of Sicily involve outrageous plot lines and famous characters, perhaps her best story was from her young days in Sicily, where Sophia and her best friend share three things: 'a pizza recipe, some dough and a dream'. Everything is going great until one day a fast-talking pepperoni salesman gallops into town. The salesman dates Sophia one night, and then her friend the next night.

Pretty soon, he drives a wedge between the girls. Before you know it, the pizza suffers, the business suffers, and the friendship suffers. The girls part company and head for America, never to see each other again. At the end of her story, Sophia reveals that the other girl turned out to be Mama Celeste, a popular American brand of frozen pizza.

Hometown Girls
Blanche in Georgia

Blanche grew up at Twin Oaks, the Devereaux family mansion built on a plantation near Atlanta, Georgia. Twin Oaks was run by her mother Elizabeth-Ann and her father Curtis, better known as 'Big Daddy'. Blanche had an idyllic childhood at Twin Oaks, and often reminisces about her upbringing and young life as a classic Southern belle, flirting with suitors and basically being doted on by everyone around her.

Twin Oaks was close to Grandview plantation, home to Blanche's grandparents, Marie and William (Grammy and Grandpappy) Hollingsworth, and where Blanche's father and uncle Lucas grew up. Blanche treasured her time at Grandview, and would often tell the other girls about the times she used to confide in her Grammy by the fireside while drinking eggnog.

When Blanche finds out Grandview is going to be sold and turned into a hotel, the girls drive all night to stop the development. Blanche handcuffs herself to the radiator in her old bedroom, but feels her Grammy is watching over her when she hears the wind chimes Grammy used to love. Blanche makes peace with losing the hotel and takes the wind chimes home with her, to hang by her bedroom window as a tribute to Grammy.

FUN FACT
Atlanta, Georgia is also significant to Dorothy, because she moves there at the end of the series after marrying Blanche's uncle Lucas — making their home at Hollingsworth Manor, not far from Twin Oaks and Grandview.

Dorothy in Brooklyn

Brooklyn, New York City is the hometown to Dorothy, where she grew up after her parents Sophia and Salvadore Petrillo emigrated to the United States during the 1920s. According to Sophia, Dorothy was conceived in Brooklyn one night in 1929 after Sophia and Salvadore had their first argument as newlyweds.

The Brooklyn neighbourhood the Petrillos lived in was a vibrant and crowded place populated by many other Italian immigrants working hard to start a new life. Sophia alludes many times to the mafia presence in her life in both Italy and Brooklyn, as well as her adherence to Sicilian customs and superstitions that were ever-present in the Petrillo home. We are taken back to Dorothy and Sophia's life in Brooklyn several times during *The Golden Girls*. In these 'back in time' episodes, Estelle Getty simply toned down Sophia's old lady makeup to appear younger, while Lynnie Greene was hired to play a younger Dorothy.

In 'One for the Money' (S03E02), we see Dorothy as a young mother trying to make ends meet. She visits Sophia to ask for babysitting help so she can take a second job.

In 'Dateline: Miami' (S07E07), the girls reminisce about old dates they've been on, and Sophia takes us back to Brooklyn in 1948 to tell the story of Dorothy's first date with Stan that resulted in an unwanted pregnancy (and let's face it – an unwanted husband!).

In 'Mother's Day' (S03E25) we are transported back to Mother's Day 1957, when Sophia and Salvadore convince Sophia's mother to move in with them. Just to make things complicated, Sophia's elderly mother is played by Bea Arthur, made up to look elderly while performing in a wheelchair. In this episode we also see Dorothy and Stan visit his mother because they need to borrow money. While it appears that Stan's mother doesn't like Dorothy, Stan leaves the room and she confides in Dorothy that she thinks Stan as a *yutz* as well, and secretly gives Dorothy twice as much money as they asked for.

In 'A Piece of Cake' (S02E25), Sophia tells the story of her birthday in Brooklyn in 1956, which she believes to be her 48th birthday, until she realises there is a mistake on her birth certificate and she is actually 50.

The Rusty Anchor

Why hello there, stranger. May I pour you a moderately priced beverage? It's always happy hour at the Rusty Anchor.

The Rusty Anchor played host to many a *Golden Girls* date night, but the most iconic Rusty Anchor moment was in 'Journey to the Center of Attention' (S07E18) when Blanche convinces Dorothy to join her for 'Nickel Beer Night' and she gets way more than she bargained for.

When they arrive, Blanche immediately ditches Dorothy for a literal conga-line of lustful men. Despondent, Dorothy takes a seat and soon strikes up a conversation with the pianist. When the pianist asks Dorothy if she can sing, she feigns ignorance for at least ten seconds before asking if he knows anything by Irving Berlin.

Shyly at first, she begins to sing 'What'll I Do?', and gradually the bar flies start paying attention. When Dorothy realises she is building an audience, she stands up and belts out the next verse to high applause from everyone in the bar. Everyone is thrilled except Blanche, who is immediately jealous. Despite informing the men that she isn't wearing a bra, Blanche is no longer the centre of attention, and she won't stand for it.

The next day, Blanche decides to go to The Rusty Anchor without her newly famous roommate. but Dorothy calls in to the bar on her way home from the laundromat and wows the crowd again, this time with her rendition of 'Hard-Hearted Hannah'.

Dorothy is enjoying the attention so much that she invites all her roommates to see her sing again the next night. Blanche begrudgingly accepts, but has an ace up the sleeve of her baggy trench coat – a sexy red dress, a plunging neckline and a secret plan to steal the show. Blanche takes to the stage and starts to sing 'I Wanna Be Loved By You', but doesn't get much love at all after a few on-stage mishaps. Her awkward microphone technique sees her nearly take out half the audience, and just when it looks like things can't get any worse, she gives a lap dance to a man who has recently had hip surgery.

Blanche runs from the stage devastated, and Dorothy runs after her so they can talk. Blanche admits she is jealous, and pays Dorothy the biggest compliment she has ever given her – that Dorothy lights up the room when she sings, and that she is beautiful. They make up, and decide to attend The Rusty Anchor on separate nights from then on so as not to step on each other's toes.

Season 6 overview

AIRED: September 1990 — May 1991
BEST EPISODES: Zborn Again • Sister of the Bride •
There Goes the Bride: Parts 1 & 2

In Season 6, there are multiple storylines that focus on the girls' extended families. Blanche's brother Clayton returns, this time with news of his pending nuptials with his boyfriend Doug. Blanche struggles with the idea at first, but the girls convince her otherwise and Blanche accepts that Clayton deserves to follow his heart and gives him her blessing.

Rose, despite believing for many years that her real father was either Bob Hope or a clown travelling with the Ringling Brothers Circus, finally meets her biological father, Brother Martin, in a serendipitous moment when he is admitted to the hospital at which she works. At first, they both think that the familiarity between them is because they both hail from St. Olaf, but when he finds out Rose's full name, he admits that he is her real father. Although she is sad that they never knew each other, Rose ultimately forgives him, because she had wonderful adoptive parents and a happy life despite never knowing him.

Blanche gets a surprise visit from Viola Watkins, her childhood nanny (or Mammy, as they say in the South). Blanche and her Mammy haven't spoken for years because Blanche felt her Mammy had abandoned her as a lonely ten-year-old child. When they meet, Viola tells Blanche an uncomfortable truth about Big Daddy. It turns out that Viola and Big Daddy had an affair when Blanche was young, forcing Viola to leave her job when Blanche's mother found out. Blanche must reckon with forgiving Viola for leaving, and ultimately forgiving Big Daddy for being unfaithful to her mother.

There are two deaths that have a major influence on the girls during Season 6. Tragically, Sophia's son (and Dorothy's brother), Phil, dies suddenly from a heart attack while trying on cheap knock-off dresses at 'Big Girls Pay Less'. Dorothy is tasked with delivering the eulogy, and Sophia must make peace with Phil's widow Angela after their long running feud, as well as her mixed feelings about Phil being a transvestite. Rose's experience as a grief counsellor comes in handy and she negotiates a truce between Sophia and Angela, and Sophia bids an emotional goodbye to her son.

CLASSIC MOMENT
Blanche coming to terms with her brother Clayton marrying his boyfriend Doug.

Another death that has a big effect on Sophia is the passing of a nun who she is close friends with. Sophia decides to pay tribute to her by following in her footsteps and becoming a nun herself. Of course, this lasts only a few days after the convent realises what a handful Sophia can be.

Stan tries to woo Dorothy by impressing her with his newfound wealth after he invented a baked-potato opener that sells like hotcakes. They have a fling, but Dorothy is in denial about getting serious. The romance escalates in 'There Goes the Bride: Parts 1 & 2', where Dorothy nearly ends up walking down the aisle with Stan for a second time. Sophia forbids it and threatens to walk out of Dorothy's life if she goes through with it. On the morning of the wedding, Sophia gives Dorothy her blessing, but the wedding is called off by Dorothy at the last minute after Stan tries to make her sign a pre-nup.

Right near the end of Season 6, in the two-part 'Never Yell Fire in a Crowded Retirement Home', the truth around the Shady Pines fire is finally revealed. Police turn up to the house to interrogate Sophia after the deathbed confession of another Shady Pines resident implicates her in the mysterious fire back in 1985. According to the report, Sophia and her friend started the fire in Sophia's room while making s'mores using a contraband hotplate. The police arrest Sophia, who is bailed out but faces trial. To avoid jail, Sophia decides to jump bail and move back to Sicily. Luckily Sophia eventually beats the charges because it turns out that the fire was actually insurance fraud, and not caused by those s'mores after all.

CLASSIC MOMENT
Dorothy coming to her senses just in time before marrying Stan again.

Episodes

The Sets
The house

The exterior of *The Golden Girls* house will be familiar to all viewers, as it was often used as the opening shot of each episode. Along with the opening theme music, the comforting sight of the Golden Girls home heralded our invitation into their lives each week. But where was the real Golden Girls house actually located?

The address of the fictional home was 6151 Richmond Street in Miami, Florida. However, the home used in the exterior shot is actually located at 245 North Saltair Avenue in the Los Angeles suburb of Brentwood, California. External shots of this home were used in the early seasons of *The Golden Girls*, with later episodes using an exact replica of the home's façade that was constructed at Disney–MGM Studios (now Disney's Hollywood Studios) in Orlando, Florida.

You can still drive past the original Golden Girls house in Brentwood; however, the Disney studio replica was torn down in 2003 after it was damaged in a hurricane. The damaged exterior was destroyed along with several others to make way for another attraction.

The Sets
The kitchen

Welcome to the kitchen. Join us at the table and take a load off. May we offer you some coffee and a slice of cheesecake?

The kitchen table was home to just about every serious conversation held between the four girls. It also hosted more than the occasional midnight-snack session, and was the place to be if you enjoyed Sophia's regular Sicilian feasts of her beloved spaghetti with marinara sauce.

You may not have noticed, but there were only ever three seats at the kitchen table. This was purely for staging reasons – four chairs would mean one of the girls would have her back to camera. To get around this, one of the girls always stood or sat on a stool when all four were in the kitchen.

While the kitchen decor stayed mostly the same throughout the series, one thing that did change very regularly was the tablecloth. The tablecloth could be matched to the outfits worn by the girls, and was often changed at the last minute if it clashed with any of the actors' wardrobe. The curtains also changed a few times during the series, but nowhere near as often as the tablecloth.

The Sets

The lanai

Welcome to our lanai. Why not sit back and luxuriate on one of our tastefully upholstered sun lounges. May I offer you a tall glass of ice-cold sweet tea?

In the hot and humid Miami climate, what home would be complete without an outdoor tropical sanctuary? The lanai offered the girls a place to enjoy the weather and soak up some sunshine, while also affording some space for private conversations.

The lanai was located behind the lounge room and was surrounded by palm trees and other tropical plants. Furniture on the lanai had a Parisian feel, and included several wrought-iron sun lounges, a matching buffet trolley and a scattering of small tables, so beverages were never too far out of reach. The girls might also use a parasol to take shelter from the Miami sun during the heat of the day.

FUN FACT
The word 'lanai' was pretty much unfamiliar to everyone outside of Miami — even Sophia admitted to not knowing what it was in an early episode. A lanai is simply an outdoor area with a cement floor and some kind of shelter from the sun. So now we all know!

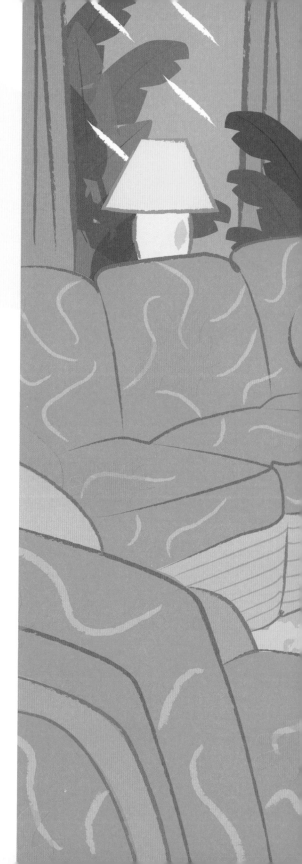

The Sets

The living room

Welcome to the Golden Girls living room. Settle down on the comfy couch, if you can find a space between the homely throw cushions and the tastefully appointed late 1980s decor.

The living room is a warm and inviting space where the girls gather to relax and host some of their guests. The living room has seen many hilarious moments over the years. We all live for Blanche's dramatic living-room entrances, head held high and sweeping across the floor in a flowing robe or gown. The living room is also home to the front door of the house, the scene of many great comedic entrances, as well as the antique Chinese vase treasured by Blanche, until Rose shoots it to pieces when aiming for an intruder that turns out to just be Blanche returning from a date.

The living room is stylishly decorated with indoor plants, cane furniture and bold upholstery fabrics. The living room takes full advantage of the Miami sun, with large areas of the ceiling made of glass to let the sun shine in. Beyond a smaller sitting area lies an open fireplace, though it's hard to imagine roasting chestnuts on an open fire in the humid Miami climate.

The Sets

Blanche's bedroom

Why hello there, sailor. Welcome to Blanche's boudoir. Pardon us while we slip into something more comfortable.

While all the girls' bedrooms are unique, Blanche's bedroom stands out as the most lavish and memorable (she is the homeowner, after all). The most striking feature is the stunning banana leaf wallpaper, giving the room a perfect tropical feel, matched by impeccable nest bed linens, a matching throw pillow or two, and tasteful white-shaded lamps on each bedside. The green colour of the banana leaf is matched with several green-hued trinkets and vases on a long table opposite the end of the bed.

Blanche's private quarters do not end at the bedroom. Like any self-respecting glamour queen, Blanche has her own ensuite bathroom, because a lady shouldn't have to leave the boudoir just to powder her nose.

When we look at Blanche's bedroom furnishings, we are reminded of what our grandmothers have always told us: what is old always becomes new again, eventually. The tropical leaf pattern is again having a moment and with a few tweaks to modernise, the decor in Blanche's bedroom wouldn't be out of place in many homes today.

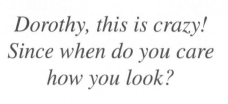

Golden Moments in Fashion

When we watch episodes of *The Golden Girls* today, one of the most striking features is the clothing worn by the cast. These were not four dowdy older women: the apparel worn by the four lead actors reflected the iconic late 1980s and early 1990s fashion trends, while also staying true to the characters' ages and maturity.

Judy Evans was the masterful costume designer for every single episode of *The Golden Girls*. For her incredible design and illustrations she received several awards during her career.

In addition to the designing the wardrobe for the girls' daytime and evening looks, Evans also created some incredible one-off novelty costumes for *The Golden Girls*. Who could forget Dorothy, Blanche and Rose starring in a children's theatre production of *Henny Penny* the musical, or Blanche and Rose rushing from their dress rehearsal to the hospital in their *Cats* costumes? The outrageous aerobics outfits designed for Blanche and Dorothy were hilarious to audiences, but really did look fantastic on them both.

Bea Arthur loved her outfit so much that she wore the sparkly aerobics top over a chic silk shirt to the Emmy Awards in 1989 and looked fabulous.

Judy Evans ensured that each of the lead actors on *The Golden Girls* had her own unique style, and tried to design clothing for each woman based not only on her character, but on the actor's personal taste. This was particularly true for Rue McClanahan and Bea Arthur, whereas Betty White and Estelle Getty had slightly less flexible costumes due to Getty's requirement to look twenty years older when playing Sophia, and White's requirement to portray the sweet and innocent Rose.

Dorothy's style

Did somebody say BIG collars? Throughout *The Golden Girls*, Dorothy's wardrobe consisted of styles that flattered the taller woman (Arthur was about 177 cm tall) during an era in which people thought it was okay to team crushed velvet with suede boots – this was no mean feat.

Dorothy wore layers, layers and more layers. She often wore long tops and structured jackets that suited her height, and teamed a neutral-coloured high-necked top with a tailored long jacket in a contrasting colour. Dorothy mixed patterns and textures of fabric, and finished the look with a long skirt and flat boots. Bea Arthur did not care for heels, so Judy Evans never made her wear them.

For evening wear, Dorothy often donned long gowns with shoulder pads, and she was certainly not shy about a sequin or two. Bold, big jewellery was a key accessory for Dorothy, including long necklaces, chunky brooches and big earrings (clip-ons only, because Bea Arthur didn't have pierced ears).

Blanche's style

There is no denying it: Blanche Devereaux is a 1980s style icon. Throughout *The Golden Girls*, Blanche's outfits were as bold and brash as the sexy southerner herself. Audiences loved seeing her glamorous and often outrageous outfits each week, and from day through to evening, Blanche oozed confidence and epitomised glamour.

Blanche was just as dazzling in bright colours and bold synthetic fabrics as she was in muted pastels and wool. Her dresses were tight enough to show off her curves, and usually had a neckline that plunged just enough to reveal her ample bosom. Blanche's accessories were always glitzy and her heels were always high.

Of course, for Blanche, dressing to impress doesn't end when she gets home at night. It shouldn't be at all surprising that one of Blanche's key looks is what she wears to bed: Blanche's sexy sleepwear is defined by the floaty gown. Rue McClanahan famously had it written into her contract that she could keep all of Blanche's attire. Her wardrobe certainly contained the stuff of fashion dreams.

Rose's style

A true devotee of the humble sweater vest, Rose's style was defined by practical outfits with a fun twist. A sweater vest with a cute design teamed with sensible slacks were the order of daytime wear for Rose – think the sweater vest with an illustrated farm scene she wore early on in the series. Rose loved a tailored pantsuit in a block colour and looked as good in pastels as she did in bolder shades.

Rose's evening look was always classy, flattering, and showed a little flair when required. Matching top-and-skirt ensembles dominated her evening wear choices, usually with a V-shaped neckline to flatter Rose's rather ample bosom without giving too much away.

Betty White was a great dancer and had a killer set of legs to show for it. Her evening wear certainly showed off plenty of her best assets, always complemented with a flattering pair of tights and some heels (or tap shoes when required).

Sophia's style

Sophia perfected grandma chic with a range of looks befitting a woman in her 80s *during* the eighties. Never one to show too much skin, high necks and slacks were key to her look, teamed with a sensible pair of flat shoes. Sophia loved a frilly collar and always buttoned to the top.

For evening wear, Sophia chose outfits that were modest but still glamorous – think pantsuits and long skirts. Like all good Italian women of her era, she also kept a go-to version of her favourite outfits in black for times of grief.

Sophia's accessories were simple and often functional – her trademark glasses could always be found on a chain around her neck. Sophia's love of cooking meant rocking a multitude of aprons over the course of the series. And who could forget THAT purse? Sophia's purse was never out of her sight. Such was her love for it, she often carried her purse with her from room to room in the house.

Season 7 overview

AIRED: September 1991 — May 1992
BEST EPISODES: Dateline: Miami • Room 7 •
Journey to the Center of Attention •
One Flew Out of the Cuckoo's Nest: Parts 1 & 2

Season 7 of *The Golden Girls* begins with a big shock: Rose finds a photo that appears to show her late husband, Charlie, in bed with Blanche. Perplexed, Rose sneaks a peak into Blanche's journal and sees that she once slept with a man named Chuck around the time that Charlie had previously visited Miami. Just as Rose is about to confront Blanche, Rose discovers that the other photos on that film had been double exposed (a very 1990s problem to have) and that Charlie and Blanche's love affair never actually happened.

In a homage to the popular TV program *Murder, She Wrote*, we see the girls participate in a murder mystery weekend that starts off as fun, but ends in a real-life stabbing. To make matters worse, Blanche becomes the prime suspect! Just when it looks like Blanche is a cold-blooded killer, the joke is on her when it is revealed that the second murder was also part of the murder mystery game.

In another prank, Sophia fools Rose in an incident that nearly convinces Rose to move out. Miles presents Rose with a friendship

ring to show his love, but Rose becomes concerned that Charlie is trying to show his disapproval from beyond the grave because of a number of 'signs'. This isn't helped by Sophia pretending to be possessed by Charlie from beyond the grave to express his negative feelings about Miles. Rose dumps Miles on the advice of Charlie's 'spirit', but Sophia feels guilty and admits it was a prank. Rose is so hurt she threatens to move out, but Sophia apologises and convinces her to get back with Miles.

Speaking of paranormal activity, in a terrifying moment for the household, the girls get a huge shock in Episode 11 when Sophia has a bad choking spell that causes her to fall unconscious. While Sophia is out cold, she has a near-death experience and meets her husband, Salvadore, in Heaven. When Sophia finally comes to, she tells Dorothy, who refuses to believe her.

Meanwhile, in the same episode, Blanche finds out that her Grammy's plantation in Atlanta is going to be sold and turned into a hotel. Blanche is devastated, so the girls drive all night to try to put a stop to the

development. Despite initially handcuffing herself to the radiator to prevent the demolition, Blanche comes to her senses and says her final goodbye to the house, souveniring her Grammy's wind chimes as a reminder of their special relationship.

In the two-part finale that ends Season 7 and *The Golden Girls* series, Blanche's uncle Lucas (played by Leslie Nielsen) visits Miami, and Blanche organises for Lucas to go on a date with Dorothy to get him out of her hair so she can go on a date with a new man. While Dorothy and Lucas are initially not particularly impressed with each other, they soon find a common interest in getting revenge on Blanche once they realise they've been set up. Dorothy and Lucas decide to fool Blanche into thinking that they have fallen in love, going so far as to tell her they are now engaged. There's just one problem: Dorothy and Lucas actually *do* fall in love, and decide to get married for real.

Meanwhile, Blanche, Rose and Sophia are deciding what to do after Dorothy leaves the house. Rose plans to move in with her daughter, while Sophia is planning to move with Dorothy and Lucas to his estate in Atlanta. But at the last minute, the three girls realise the strength of their friendship, and it occurs to them that they are each other's family now and should keep living together in Miami. Despite a last-minute diversion for Dorothy on the way to the wedding caused by Stan (a sweet moment where Stan disguises himself as a limo driver to give his blessing), Dorothy marries Lucas and couldn't be happier. But with this joy comes sadness, as Dorothy must say goodbye to the other girls and move to Atlanta, bringing this much-loved series to a close.

CLASSIC MOMENT
Dorothy finally finding true
love and marrying Lucas.

Episodes

Golden Gamechangers

How one sitcom confronted topical storylines and changed TV forever

The 1980s and 1990s were sitcom glory days, with hundreds of television shows competing for viewers and advertising dollars. While many sitcoms came and went, *The Golden Girls* enjoyed early and sustained success, and has never really been out of syndication. While *The Golden Girls* is beloved for its humour and its great characters, it's easy to forget just how unique and ground-breaking the show was for its time.

There is no doubt *The Golden Girls* changed the landscape of American television as we know it. In 1985, there were no other TV shows that centred around four women – let alone four women over the age of fifty. *The Golden Girls* was not only a well-written comedy, but it also raised issues that many other light entertainment programs at the time wouldn't touch.

Although mainstream audiences found much of *The Golden Girls* to be familiar and relatable, many episodes courted controversy by covering a litany of topics that were largely taboo for a late-1980s television audience.

Topical, hard-hitting issues like HIV/AIDS were challenging to cover in a 30-minute primetime comedy, but the writers managed to skilfully weave them into the storyline, informing viewers about topics many hadn't been exposed to. It is also worth noting that controversial storylines weren't just reserved for guest stars – the central characters all experienced direct involvement in these challenging themes.

Racism

Unfortunately, racism was still fairly rife on TV shows in the late 1980s. Like many other programs of the era, *The Golden Girls* was not immune to the occasional racist joke, which wouldn't pass muster on television today, but the show did confront racism in a positive manner on a few occasions.

In 'Dorothy's New Friend' (S03E15), Dorothy befriends Miami author Barbara Thorndyke (played by Bonnie Bartlett). While Barbara seems to be Dorothy's intellectual match, she behaves condescendingly towards Blanche and Rose. Dorothy is initially unaware of Barbara's character flaws, but her true self is revealed when Barbara refuses to attend dinner with Sophia's date Murray Guttman (played by Monty Ash, 1909–1998) because Jews aren't allowed at the Mortimer Club where Barbara is a member. Dorothy chastises Barbara for being anti-Semitic and so cruel to the other girls, and promptly shows her the door, ending their friendship.

Suicide

The issue of suicide is raised in 'Not Another Monday' (S05E07, where we meet Sophia's friend Martha Lamont (played by Geraldine Fitzgerald, 1913–2005). Martha suffers terribly from physical pain and loneliness and tells Sophia about her plans to end her own life. Sophia is shocked when Martha asks her to hold her hand while she takes the pills, but decides to support her friend and agrees to go along with Martha's plan. The girls try to convince Sophia not to get involved because of the trauma she might experience, but Sophia insists on helping her friend. Sophia arrives at Martha's house but at the last minute, delivers a speech to Martha about why she thinks life is still worth living. Sophia convinces her that she will always be there to support her, and thankfully, Martha decides not to go through with it.

Sexual assault

Sexual assault was another sensitive topic rarely broached in sitcoms at the time. In *Feelings* (S06E06), Rose returns from a dental appointment very upset after suspecting her dentist touched her breasts during the anaesthesia and made lewd comments about her figure.

The girls convince Rose to confront the dentist. He initially convinces her it is all in her head, and tricks her into apologising for her misunderstanding. He proceeds with another check-up, but it doesn't take long for him to make more lewd comments about her body. Rose finally realises she was right all along and gives him a serious telling off, adding that she will report him to the State Dental Board.

LGBTIQ issues

Homosexuality was a recurrent theme across the lifespan of *The Golden Girls*, with a lesbian storyline centred around Dorothy's friend Jean in the second season, as well as the introduction of Blanche's gay 'baby' brother, Clayton, who we meet in 'Scared Straight' (S04E09), when he visits Miami to spend time with his sister. A closeted homosexual, Clayton was formerly married to a woman, but they broke up as he could no longer continue living a lie.

Clayton considers coming out to Blanche, but is worried about her reaction. He confides his secret to Rose – and then claims to have slept with her, in order to protect his secret. Eventually, he tells Blanche the truth, and while she initially doesn't know how to respond, she realises that he is still the same baby brother she has always loved dearly, and she wants Clayton to be happy. In a later episode, Clayton returns to Miami to tell Blanche that he is marrying his partner Doug, and while Blanche is upset at first, the other girls convince her that she must accept Clayton for who he is.

HIV/AIDS

In 1990, there was no more sensitive topic than HIV/AIDS. It was still the early days of the disease in America, and many members of the community remained misinformed and fearful, particularly around gay men and their potential to spread the disease. The episode '72 Hours' (S05E19) was one of the first storylines about HIV/AIDS on television, and aimed to educate viewers and dispel some of the myths surrounding the disease.

The episode is centred around Rose, who fears she may have contracted HIV via a contaminated blood transfusion when having her gall bladder removed six years earlier. The girls rally around Rose and discuss the disease in ways that were clearly trying to send a message to the public. The show dismantles the myth of transmission by touch, or from sharing a bathroom with someone, as well as encouraging people to practise safe sex, using Blanche's regrets about the risks she has taken as an example that HIV was not just a homosexual disease. The episode also encouraged parents to discuss the dangers of HIV with their children.

Thankfully it all works out in the end for Rose and she gets a clean bill of health, but this episode was ground-breaking and helped to educate audiences of all ages.

Drug addiction

In 'High Anxiety' (S04E20), Sophia accidentally knocks a bottle of Rose's pills down the sink, and the girls notice Rose's mood swings when the pills could not be replaced straight away. Suspicious, they confront Rose, and learn that she is addicted to the painkillers that she had started taking thirty years earlier after a plough-pulling injury in St. Olaf. The girls insist that Rose give up the pills and she soon goes into withdrawal. The girls stay up all night in solidarity with Rose, and she manages to go 24 hours without a painkiller. Unfortunately, it isn't so simple for Rose, and she eventually takes more painkillers to get through the day.

Rose realises that she needs help, and even though the girls are a great support, she seeks professional help. The episode ends with Rose admitting that she is an addict, but she is also optimistic about being able to fight her addiction with the support of Narcotics Anonymous and her friends.

Elder care

The challenges faced by older people finding appropriate housing and care is often considered in *The Golden Girls*. In 'Sophia's Choice' (S04E22), Sophia's friend Lillian (played by Ellen Albertini Dow, 1913–2015) moves from Shady Pines to Sunny Pastures, a retirement facility that Sophia thinks is even worse than the dreaded Shady Pines. Sophia soon rescues Lillian by inviting her to stay at the house, but the girls soon realise Lillian requires full-time care that they are unable to provide.

Dorothy and Sophia visit Sunny Pastures to convince them to do better by their residents, but it turns out that the staff aren't to blame – Sunny Pastures receives poor government funding and is already running at a loss. Rose finds a better facility, but Lillian's benefits don't quite cover the cost of staying there. As the girls wonder how to come up with the money, Blanche comes to the rescue by providing the cash she was saving for breast augmentation to see that Lillian has at least two years of accommodation covered for.

Homelessness

Just as it is today, homelessness was a big issue in the late 1980s and early 1990s, with more than three million homeless people in the United States. In 'Brother, Can You Spare That Jacket?' (S04E08), Blanche wins $10,000 on a lottery ticket that goes missing when Sophia donates Blanche's jacket to the thrift store, which contains the ticket in its pocket. Unbelievably (outside of a sitcom, at least), the jacket is bought by Michael Jackson, who wears it in a performance and donates it to charity. The jacket is then bought by a local congressman, who donates it to a local homeless shelter. Blanche, Rose, Dorothy and Sophia spend the night at the shelter, where each has a meaningful conversation with a homeless person. Blanche eventually finds the ticket, but the girls decide to donate all the money to the homeless shelter after being touched by their stories.

The girls have another meaningful experience with the homeless in 'Have Yourself a Very Little Christmas' (S05E12). In this episode, the girls decide to volunteer at Rose's church, which is supplying a meal for the homeless on Christmas Day. The girls are sad to see several children present at the dinner, and wish they could help them more. In a lesson that aims to educate the audience, the priest tells them all about the lack of affordable housing in the area, and how rents are going up and the minimum wage isn't increasing in the United States.

Stan also visits the shelter after finding himself homeless when his wife kicks him out and his latest money-making scheme (ordering toy fire engines from Germany to sell as Christmas gifts) fell through after the toys failed to arrive in Miami until Christmas Eve. Dorothy convinces Stan to stop wallowing in self-pity, because he has always managed to turn things around in the past. The episode ends in a touching moment when Stan returns to the shelter dressed as Santa Claus with armfuls of toy fire engines for the children.

Problem gambling

In 'All Bets Are Off' (S05E24), Rose takes an interest in painting, and Dorothy takes Rose to the horse track when she needs some real-life inspiration to paint a horse. When Sophia finds out that Dorothy has been to the track, she is horrified, and we learn that Dorothy had a gambling addiction 15 years earlier.

Dorothy promises that it was a one-off, but Sophia is suspicious when she finds Dorothy reading the form guide. Later, we see Dorothy postponing a job interview in order to place a bet, and Sophia's worst fears are confirmed when she searches through Dorothy's purse and finds betting slips. It turns out that years earlier, Dorothy had gotten herself into trouble with loan sharks, and Sophia had to pay them off by cashing in Salvadore's life insurance. Rose convinces Dorothy to seek help, and she returns to Gamblers Anonymous, vowing to fight her problem one day at a time.

Welcome to
The Golden Palace

At the end of *The Golden Girls*, we see Blanche, Sophia and Rose say goodbye to Dorothy and take over the running of a flailing Miami hotel. The Golden Palace Hotel is in a bit of a sorry state – most of the previous staff have left, leaving the girls to take on many of the jobs around the hotel to make ends meet.

Blanche runs the hotel, while Sophia is co-chef in the hotel's restaurant. Rose is the hotel's 'jack of all trades', and finds herself doing everything from cooking and cleaning to receiving guests. Cheech Marin (from comedy duo Cheech and Chong) starred as the hotel's chef, a role originally planned for English comedian Alexei Sayle.

A few familiar faces turn up to visit the girls at The Golden Palace. Miles Webber, Rose's long-time boyfriend from the original series, arrives to visit Rose, but brings with him a shocking secret: his name is found in the hotel registry dating back several years, suggesting that he has been unfaithful. (We never liked him since he put the moves on Dorothy anyway!)

The Golden Palace also saw the return of Dorothy, who comes to visit the hotel during a two-part episode. While pleased to see her mother and to catch up with her old friends, Dorothy is concerned that Sophia is working too hard at the hotel. This culminates in a trip to Shady Pines, where Sophia realises that the retirement home isn't as bad as she once thought it was.

Even Dorothy's ex-husband, Stan, shows up, despite being presumed dead. Sophia becomes suspicious that Stan has faked his own death to evade taxes because she keeps seeing him around the hotel. The other girls think Sophia is losing her marbles, but Sophia is convinced it is him. We never do find out if Stan is a figment of her imagination, or not.

The Golden Palace only lasted a single season due to poor ratings, with the finale seeing Sophia finally move back to the Shady Pines retirement home for good.

The Ultimate
Golden Girls quiz

Think you know your way around every episode of
The Golden Girls? Want to find out if you're a solid gold
fan of the greatest TV show of all time? Test your knowledge
right this minute with the ultimate Golden Girls quiz!

1. Who was the youngest actress in *The Golden Girls* house?

2. Which famous artist did Sophia claim to have had an affair with?

3. What was the code name for sex that Dorothy and Lucas created?

4. What weapon does Ray's jealous ex-wife use to attack Rose with after Rose and Ray go out for dinner at a seafood restaurant?

5. What address do the Golden Girls live at?

6. What kind of fruit does Sophia routinely catch a bus to purchase?

7. Name the original artist who wrote 'Thank You for Being a Friend'.

8. How many guys did Rose have flings with in St. Olaf before Charlie?

9. How many chairs were there in the girls' kitchen?

10. Which song does Blanche sing during her big moment at The Rusty Anchor?

11. Which character's husband died while they were making love?

12. What is Blanche's maiden name?

13. What were the girls breeding in their garage to make some extra cash?

14. In which year did the final episode of *The Golden Girls* air?

15. What is the name of the dog that saved Rose's family from a house fire?

16. What three-letter word does Blanche's initials spell out?

17. Which Golden Girl gets to compete in an episode of *Jeopardy*?

18. What illegal leisure item was Blanche hiding in the house without a permit?

19. What item is sent to Sophia from Sicily that she interprets as a vendetta?

20. The dentist in St. Olaf also had another career. What was it?

1. Rue McClanahan (Blanche) 2. Pablo Picasso 3. Freddy Peterson 4. A lobster 5. 6151 Richmond Street 6. A nectarine 7. Andrew Gold 8. 56 9. Three 10. 'I Wanna Be Loved By You' 11. Rose 12. Hollingsworth 13. Minks 14. 1992 15. Rusty 16. B.E.D. 17. Dorothy 18. A hot tub 19. A black feather 20. Librarian

Golden Girls are doing it for themselves

A feminist sitcom about four independent women

The Golden Girls is a uniquely feminist story about self-sufficient older women and the unique problems and triumphs they face. While the show did have a significant focus on the women's dating lives, the recurring theme was that the women didn't really need men after all, and they always returned to each other's friendship in the end.

Before *The Golden Girls*, sitcoms that dealt with feminist issues were rare. A decade earlier, the sitcom *Maude* (running from 1972 to 1978) set the feminist benchmark for television programs, addressing many women's issues including abortion, domestic violence and gender equality at a time when these issues were considered 'too hot to handle' on prime-time television. *Maude* and *The Golden Girls* are of course linked in many ways – Bea Arthur starred in the titular role and Rue McClanahan had a supporting role in the series. *The Golden Girls* creator Susan Harris also wrote four episodes of *Maude*, including the two-part episode where Maude Findlay has an abortion.

From the first episode, the show's major theme was the strength of the girls' collective friendship. When Blanche's wedding is called off, she reveals that despite thinking that the marriage was her last hope at happiness, she realised she was actually still very happy. Blanche tells the girls, 'You made the difference – you're my family, and you make me happy to be alive.' The girls embrace, with Dorothy vowing that they would all stick together, no matter what. And over the next seven seasons, the girls lived and breathed this mantra.

The feminist theme of self-sufficiency is established very early. In 'Break In' (S01E08), the girls are on edge after returning home from a Madonna concert to find that they've been robbed. This is exactly the kind of situation that might make them wish a man had been in the house to protect them, and initially, they reminisce about having husbands to make them feel safe. After spending a few days going security-mad with a guard dog, a burglar alarm and Blanche accidentally macing herself, Rose crosses the line and

buys a gun. After Rose accidentally fires a shot at Blanche's antique vase, they realise the only thing they have to fear is fear itself and that they can take care of themselves. In 'Second Motherhood' (S01E19), the girls are having trouble finding a plumber that will give them a fair quote. When Dorothy refuses the exorbitant price quoted by one plumber and suggests they could do the job themselves, the plumber taunts her, suggesting that 'you ladies are going into your feminist phase a little late'. Dorothy realises that Rose has a decent knowledge of plumbing after growing up on a farm, and they decide to tackle the job themselves. Of course, it wouldn't be a sitcom without an ensuing string of errors as Rose takes to the bathroom haphazardly with a wrench. After a week of disasters, the plumber turns up and mocks them again, telling them they simply need a man to get the job done. But eventually Rose and Dorothy finish the job and the plumber has to eat his words.

This theme of women not being taken seriously is continued during Season 5's powerful two-part episode, 'Sick and Tired'. Dorothy has been sick and exhausted for months, but multiple doctors say there's nothing wrong with her. A Miami doctor tells her it's all in her head, and she should just 'change her hair colour' to cheer herself up; she travels to New York to see a neurologist, but even he says it's all in her head. Finally, Dorothy finds a doctor who is able to

diagnose her illness: she has chronic fatigue syndrome. This episode was written by Susan Harris to raise awareness about the condition after Harris herself endured misdiagnosed chronic fatigue for years. In the end, Dorothy runs into one of the doctors who dismissed her and confronts him about not treating her concerns seriously. As Dorothy so perfectly puts it: 'I suspect, had I been a man, I might have been taken a little bit more seriously and not told to go to a hairdresser.' Go Dorothy!

Economic security was another recurring theme, with the girls oftssen having to go to great lengths to make ends meet. While it's easy now to be cynical about the idea of four white women living in a huge house in Miami being represented as 'poor', in sitcom world at the time, nobody else was talking about the realities of making ends meet as an older single woman. Throughout the series, the women rarely had permanent work, often forced to take odd jobs or come up with money-making schemes to get by.

Few TV shows explored the dating lives of older women, and they certainly didn't go into any detail about their sexual desires. While Blanche had this more than covered, the other girls all knew what they wanted and how to get it, even if things didn't always go exactly to plan. Even Sophia, at least two decades older than the others, got her share of action.

In 'The Artist' (S03E13), Blanche introduces the girls to Laszlo, a handsome artist from the museum where she works. The girls are all very impressed by Laszlo, and Blanche is thrilled when he asks her to pose naked for his latest sculpture, to be inspired by 'the mature woman'. One by one, Laszlo convinces the other girls to sit for him as well. When the girls attend the exhibition, they find a beautiful statue that they can all see themselves in. Laszlo reveals that he took the best features of each, making the perfect woman. While there were more than a few wisecracks shared between the girls as they vied for Laszlo's attention, this episode showed a group of older women confident and comfortable with their sexuality and empowered in their own skin.

Women's rights issues were expertly woven into many storylines. In 'That's for Me to Know' (S07E04), it is revealed that Sophia was married once before her husband Salvadore. After Dorothy finds a mysterious wedding photograph with her mother standing next to an unfamiliar man, Sophia reveals that back in Sicily, when she was only fourteen, her parents arranged for her to marry a man from her village. Fearing a life with a man she didn't love, she had the marriage annulled and emigrated to the US instead. While Dorothy is initially upset that her mother had kept such a big secret, she soon realises that going against centuries

of tradition in her family was a very painful decision for Sophia and praises her as a pioneer of women's rights.

Without a doubt, *The Golden Girls* paved the way for television shows with all-women casts. Just a year after *The Golden Girls* first aired, CBS aired the first episode of *Designing Women*, a sitcom about four women and one man who run an interior design firm in Atlanta, Georgia. It's no secret that *Designing Women* was made due to the success of *The Golden Girls*. It's also easy to draw a line from *The Golden Girls* to *Sex and the City* – one of the most popular TV shows with an all-woman cast ever made. The parallels between sex-kitten Samantha and Blanche can't be ignored, nor can comparisons between innocent Charlotte and Rose. In fact, Dorothy is a total Miranda, which leaves Sophia as the Carrie – I guess three out of four ain't bad!

In the final episode of *The Golden Girls*, the emotional farewell reveals the strength and depth of the friendship shared between Dorothy, Blanche, Rose and Sophia. Although the girls initially plan to go their separate ways after Dorothy moves out, they realise that after so long, they really are each other's family, and they should stay together after all. The final powerful scene where they all embrace before Dorothy leaves says everything about the strength of friendship between these four amazing feminist women.

Published in 2019 by Smith Street Books
Melbourne | Australia
smithstreetbooks.com

ISBN: 978-1-925811-22-3

Publisher: Paul McNally
Project editor: Hannah Koelmeyer
Editor: Katri Hilden
Design: Alissa Dinallo
Illustration: Chantel de Sousa, The Illustration Room
Proofreader: Pam Dunne

Printed & bound in China by C&C Offset Printing Co., Ltd.

Book 100
10 9 8 7 6 5 4 3 2 1

Please note: This book is in no way affiliated with the creators or
copyright holders of *The Golden Girls*. We're just really big fans.
Please don't sue us.